ADDRESSING

TEST
ANXIETY

IN A HIGH-STAKES ENVIRONMENT

ADDRESSING

TEST ANXIETY

IN A HIGH-STAKES ENVIRONMENT

Gregory J. Cizek
Samantha S. Burg

STRATEGIES FOR CLASSROOMS AND SCHOOLS

CORWIN PRESS
A SAGE Publications Company
Thousand Oaks, California

For information:

Corwin Press
A Sage Publications Company
2455 Teller Road
Thousand Oaks, California 91320
www.corwinpress.com

Sage Publications Ltd
1 Oliver's Yard
55 City Road
London EC1Y 1SP
United Kingdom

Sage Publications India Pvt. Ltd.
B-42, Panchsheel Enclave
Post Box 4109
New Delhi 110 017 India

Printed in the United States of America

Library of Congress Cataloging-in-Publication Data

Cizek, Gregory J.
Addressing test anxiety in a high-stakes environment : strategies for classrooms and schools / Gregory J. Cizek, Samantha S. Burg.
    p. cm.
Includes bibliographical references and index.
ISBN 1-4129-0889-2 (cloth) — ISBN 1-4129-0890-6 (pbk.)
    1. Test anxiety—United States. I. Burg, Samantha S. II. Title.
LB3060.6.C59 2006
371.26′01′9—dc22

                                2005003644

This book is printed on acid-free paper.

05 06 07 08 09 10 9 8 7 6 5 4 3 2 1

Acquisitions editor:	Rachel Livsey
Editorial assistant:	Phyllis Cappello
Production editor:	Sanford Robinson
Copy editor:	Todd Manza, Freelance Editorial Services
Typesetter:	C&M Digitals (P) Ltd.
Proofreader:	Colleen Brennan
Cover designer:	Rose Storey
Indexer:	Karen A. McKenzie

Contents

Preface

In terms of test anxiety we, the authors of this book, are probably not much different from any of our readers. We are not clinical or experimental psychologists who have devoted a lifetime to the study of anxiety, although we have devoted some study and attention to trying to understand the phenomenon and its effects and have worked to reduce the harmful effects of test anxiety (we describe these later in the book) on students, teachers, test scores, etc. The breadth of our experience and expertise includes developing our own classroom assessments as teachers, assisting in the development and analysis of statewide achievement tests for elementary and secondary school students, and managing large-scale testing programs for professional licensure and certification. We think it is important that we have been teachers in elementary and secondary schools, having taught all subjects in second and fourth grade (GJC) and high school mathematics (SSB). Thus, we think we have much in common with fellow educators who might read this book.

Although we believe that we have a lot in common with readers, we recognize that one characteristic the two of us as authors share distinguishes us somewhat from most readers. The truth is that we consider ourselves to be specialists in educational assessment.

As testing specialists we might formally be labeled as a specific kind of social scientist known as a psychometrician. A psychometrician is a person whose specialty is **psychometrics,** which is the study of the development, administration, and interpretation of assessments. In short, we like **tests.** We will confess a position that might differentiate us from some other educators (and many students): we think that, by and large, testing is a good thing.

That said, we also think we have enough of a grasp on life in classrooms—both as students and as fellow teachers—to know that our affections for the area of educational testing are somewhat rare. We recognize that our interest in testing and an enjoyment of working with data, formulas, and so on are not characteristics that are widely shared or, perhaps, even much valued, at least in the hierarchy that makes one socially desirable. To be sure, we have heard all the jokes about testing specialists. For example:

Question: "Why did the person become a psychometrician?"

Answer: "Because he didn't have enough personality to be an accountant."

In short, we are aware that our interest in testing is something that distinguishes us from a lot of other social scientists, educators, and just plain folk. However, while we may be different from many educators in that we have some special expertise and advanced training in the field of testing, we believe that, overall, our experiences with testing and anxiety are more similar to than different from those of our readers. We still take tests. We get nervous when we are faced with a test. And we are aware that, increasingly, more and more of us are faced with more and more tests.

In this book, we try to combine our common personal experiences with testing and our professional understanding of testing and test anxiety. We think that testing and test anxiety are generally misunderstood. We think the case for the benefits of testing has too often gone unarticulated. We think, too, that the potential for test anxiety to militate against realizing those benefits is real and, to a large extent, preventable. Although test anxiety and its effects are real, we believe that we can offer some hope for educators, parents, and students by addressing test anxiety and the problems it causes.

Based on our conversations with other professionals, we believe that our readers—teachers, school counselors, school psychologists, administrators, school board members, parents, and others—share our concern. We hope to provide straightforward explanations, practical suggestions, and reasonable recommendations for addressing test anxiety in an educational environment in which tests are more prevalent and the consequences associated with testing are more important.

However, although we have attempted to write a helpful, practical book, we also did not want to underestimate the professional knowledge that our audience already possesses. Educators (and others) today are more savvy and informed about testing than ever before. Educational practice increasingly requires professionals to be familiar with research and to make data-based decisions. Thus, we have decided to try to write a book that is somewhere between a how-to checklist and a more formal academic work. We believe that our readers not only will want to know what to do about test anxiety but also will want to really *understand* the phenomenon and to grasp its underlying features, concepts, and so on.

Along those lines, we recognize that at some points we have elaborated at length on certain key concepts related to testing. We are convinced that, like many phenomena, test anxiety can exert its effects most insidiously when accurate information is unavailable or when inaccurate beliefs are widely held. It certainly is understandable that many parents, educators, and students would be apprehensive about testing to the extent that the tests they face are not well understood in terms of their purpose, their quality, or the information they provide. To that end, we believe that one of the most effective steps that educators can take to reduce test anxiety is to themselves become more informed about testing and to assist others in doing so.

The remainder of this book is organized into seven chapters. In Chapter 1, we provide some context and rationale for a book on test anxiety; we briefly define the concept of test anxiety; and we explain why we believe that our treatment of the topic is timely and important. In Chapter 2, we elaborate on what test anxiety is (and isn't) and why it should not be ignored. In Chapters 3 and 4, we provide some background information on what is known about the prevalence, correlates, and effects of test anxiety, drawing most heavily on the accumulated research knowledge on these topics. Chapter 5 provides a (very) light introduction for those who are interested in measuring test anxiety (yes, there are *tests* for test anxiety!). A companion appendix to Chapter 5 provides considerably more detail on this topic for the reader who wishes to find out more about tests that can be used to measure students' levels of test anxiety.

Chapter 6 presents some practical information about what can be done about test anxiety. Because everyone involved can play a role, this chapter presents suggestions for students, parents, teachers, educational administrators, and school systems. Chapter 7 gives brief, final words, conclusions, and recommendations.

As you may have noticed already, certain key words appear in **bold face** type. Each of these specialized terms is defined in a glossary that is included as Appendix A. An annotated compilation of some potentially helpful resources related to test anxiety is included as Appendix B. The companion material linked to Chapter 5, which provides additional information on tests that are useful for measuring levels of test anxiety, is found in Appendix C. Finally, throughout the book, important facts, definitions, or concepts are set apart and highlighted as Key Ideas.

Regarding our role in preparing this book, we must be quick to admit that the two listed authors of this book are only a minority of those who have contributed greatly to its production. We must acknowledge the many generous colleagues in the fields of education, psychology, and school counseling who have provided personal assistance or who have contributed to the theoretical or research literatures upon which we have heavily leaned. We appreciate the support for this work provided by Paula Hinton, reference librarian, and by the University Research Council at the University of North Carolina, Chapel Hill. We are grateful for the encouragement to produce this book and the helpful suggestions along the way provided by Rachel Livsey at Corwin Press, which has a long and successful history of publishing practical, helpful works in the field of education. We also appreciate the helpful editorial assistance of Phyllis Cappello, Todd Manza, and Sanford Robinson.

Finally, we want to express our appreciation for the personal encouragement and support provided by close companions and colleagues. I (SSB) would like to thank my family, Bill and JeAnne Burg and Tim and Karen Burg, for their unwavering support, love, and encouragement. I'd also like to thank my friends Jesus, Terri, Vanessa, and Spencer, who have been gentle reminders that it's not all about me. And I (GJC) acknowledge the continuing support of my wife, Rita, and our children, Caroline, A. J., David, and Stephen, who I join in thanking God for showering his abundance on the American educational system and in pleading his continuing favor.

GJC SSB
Chapel Hill, NC

The contributions of the following reviewers are gratefully acknowledged:

John M. Vitto
School Psychologist
Director of Pupil Services
Canfield, OH

Michael A. Power
Director of Instruction and Assessment
Mercer Island School District
Mercer Island, WA

Steve Hutton
On Loan to the Kentucky Department of Education's Highly
Skilled Educator Program
Villa Hills, KY

James Kelleher
Assistant Superintendent for Curriculum, Instruction & Staff
Development
Scituate Public Schools
Scituate, MA

Marcella Emberger
Director
Maryland Assessment Consortium
Baltimore, MD

Libia S. Gil
Senior Fellow
American Institutes for Research
Washington, D.C.

Theresa Rouse
Assessment and Program Evaluation Coordinator
Monterey County Office of Education
Salinas, CA

**CORWIN
PRESS**

The Corwin Press logo—a raven striding across an open book—represents the union of courage and learning. Corwin Press is committed to improving education for all learners by publishing books and other professional development resources for those serving the field of PreK–12 education. By providing practical, hands-on materials, Corwin Press continues to carry out the promise of its motto: **"Helping Educators Do Their Work Better."**

About the Authors

Gregory J. Cizek is Professor of Educational Measurement at the University of North Carolina, Chapel Hill. His background in the field of educational assessment includes five years as a manager of licensure and certification testing programs for American College Testing (ACT) in Iowa City, Iowa, and 15 years of teaching experience at the college level, where his teaching assignments have consisted primarily of graduate courses in educational testing, research methods, and statistics. He is the author of over 200 books, chapters, articles, conference papers, and reports. His books include *Handbook of Educational Policy* (Academic Press, 1998); *Cheating on Tests: How to Do It, Detect It, and Prevent It* (Lawrence Erlbaum, 1999); *Setting Performance Standards: Concepts, Methods, and Perspectives* (Lawrence Erlbaum, 2001); and *Detecting and Preventing Classroom Cheating* (Corwin Press, 2003).

Dr. Cizek has served as an elected member and vice president of a local school board in Ohio, and he currently works with several states, organizations, and the U.S. Department of Education on technical and policy issues related to large-scale standards-based testing programs for students in grades K–12. He began his career as an elementary school teacher in Michigan, where he taught second and fourth grades.

Samantha S. Burg is a doctoral student in Educational Psychology, Measurement, and Evaluation at the University of North Carolina, Chapel Hill. She holds a BS degree in engineering from the University of Oklahoma and an MA degree in mathematics education from the University of Georgia. Prior to beginning her doctoral program, she worked in the field of petroleum engineering in Alaska, served as a youth minister in Scotland, and taught high school mathematics in Georgia. Most recently, she has worked as a test development specialist for the state testing program in North Carolina.

Ms. Burg first became interested in test anxiety when she was a student teacher and her class refused to take a test; this interest has persisted throughout her doctoral research, some of which examines the ways in which test anxiety may be transmitted in classrooms. Currently, she is a research assistant on a mathematics education project and is very much interested in completing her doctoral work soon, in order to support her tennis-ball-obsessed dog, Spencer, in the fashion to which he has become accustomed. Ms. Burg has presented her research at various professional conferences and is a member of the National Council on Measurement in Education.

1

Testing in a High-Stakes Environment

It's everywhere.

Without question, testing is expanding at every level of education and into every corner of social and vocational enterprise. With that expansion has come a proliferation of test anxiety.

Test anxiety is one of those concepts that, perhaps, needs no formal introduction. We all know what test anxiety is. We have almost certainly seen or experienced its effects. We will define test anxiety more precisely and more elaborately in Chapter 2, but for the time being we think that a succinct definition will suffice. **Test anxiety** is one of many specific forms of anxiety; it results in a combination of cognitive and physical responses that are aroused in testing situations or in similar situations in which a person believes that he or she is being personally evaluated.

Of course, test anxiety itself is not a new phenomenon. It has taken on increased importance, however, as the amount of testing and the consequences associated with testing have increased, particularly in the context of K–12 education in the United States. To begin to understand the nature and effects of test anxiety, we must first consider the growth of testing in American schools.

O—🗝   **Key Idea #1   Test Anxiety . . .**

- is a specific form of anxiety;
- is prompted by situations in which a person believes that he or she is being personally evaluated; and
- results in a combination of cognitive and physical responses.

Testing and Test Anxiety in "The Good Old Days"

In the not-too-distant past, testing in schools was largely classroom-focused, comparatively informal, and had only mild consequences associated. This kind of testing calls to mind a weekly list of 10 spelling words, in which the biggest challenge for students was remembering when to change *y* to *i* before adding *es* to form a plural, or memorizing the rule about *i* coming before *e* except after *c* or when sounded like *a* as in *neighbor* or *weigh*.

For students, situations like the one just described may have induced some stress as the time came on Friday afternoon when they would have to write out the 10 plurals or decide whether it should be *receive* or *recieve*. The consequences may have seemed somewhat serious, too, for example, if the spelling test counted toward one's grade. But even a grade of F on one week's test could be ameliorated or relegated to fleeting relevance by a better performance on the list of words for the next week, or the next, or the next. . . .

For a student's parents, there were consequences of these tests, too, but they were comparatively mild. On tests such as the low-stakes spelling quiz, a parent might be affected the night before the test by flipping through flash cards with *family* on one side and *families* on the other. (Depending on the student's performance on the test the next day, perhaps more flash-card flipping would be in order.) However, parents, teachers, principals, superintendents, and others were essentially unaffected by most of the routine testing of the day.

Of course, more formal tests may also have been administered in those days. Many schools have long traditions of administering the Iowa Tests of Basic Skills (ITBS) or a similar **standardized, norm-referenced, achievement test** that provided American school children with regular training in using Number 2 pencils to color in small circles corresponding to "the one best answer."

But the consequences associated with tests like the ITBS were also minimal. Results from those tests were not regularly used to promote or retain a student. They didn't count toward a grade in a course. In fact, they really didn't "count" at all. If a test is seen as valuable enough to supplant classroom instructional time, then it would seem important for the test results to be used for some important purpose. Regrettably, however, the results from formal norm-referenced tests were often not used for anything at all. Sure, parents might get a summary of scores, such as percentile ranks (PRs), stanines, grade equivalent (GE) scores, or normal curve equivalent (NCE) scores for their individual students, although they often did—and still do—find them hard to understand. Typically, they relied on their child's teacher to interpret whether those scores meant that the child was on track, and they did not necessarily use that information for any specific purpose.

A teacher might receive a class summary report with a more complete slew of quantification—more percentiles and stanines—for every student in his or her class. Those scores may have been just as difficult for teachers to understand, and these norm-referenced test scores, once reported and explained to parents, often had no further use.

Although the data yielded by such tests *could* have been informative—and we believe that such tests continue to have the potential to provide very useful information—the fact is that the results also could largely be ignored. The absence of consequences made the results easy to overlook. For the most part, no important decision, action, grade, penalty, or reward hinged on the results.

Testing in Contemporary Education and Society

What a difference a day makes! In contrast to the low-stakes picture of the past we have just painted stands a present day in which testing seems to be omnipresent, and the importance and consequences associated with test performance are ever-increasing for all concerned.

As one example, we note the recent emphasis that legislators and policymakers have placed on ensuring that every child enters school "ready to learn." The very concept of *school readiness* suggests that some way of measuring differences in readiness among young children is necessary. Because any system for gauging those differences in school readiness is essentially a test—whether by observation, by interview, or by individually administered or group-readiness screening—the potential for test anxiety for young children (and their parents) is present.

⊙──ᴨ   **Key Idea #2   Testing in American Schools**

A report by the research arm of the U.S. Congress, the General Accounting Office (GAO), investigated the extent and cost of systemwide (i.e., state- and district-level) testing in 1993. The GAO estimated that

- the total number of individual tests administered in elementary and secondary schools each year is 36 million;
- the per-pupil cost of testing is about $14.50 per student; and
- the amount of time devoted to systemwide student testing each year is, somewhat surprisingly, only about 3.5 hours per year.

These figures predate the enactment of NCLB, which has undoubtedly served to increase extent of and expenditures on testing.

SOURCE: U.S. General Accounting Office (1993).

Regarding school testing, we also must mention the massive increase in testing prompted by the federal government. The enactment of the No Child Left Behind Act (NCLB) in 2002 has mandated annual testing in reading, mathematics, and science for every student in Grades 3 through 8 and at one point during high school, as well as monitoring of yearly progress for all schools. This immediate and far-reaching increase in testing has caused states and testing companies to scramble to meet the law's demands. As a result, it has also caused some members of the psychometric profession to jokingly refer to the federal legislation as the No Testing Specialist Left Unemployed Act.

Whereas there are essentially no consequences associated with NCLB for students, there clearly are consequences for educators and school systems who must annually report on the results of these tests. Such public disclosures present the potential for anxiety about rising or falling performance levels, graduation rates, achievement gaps, and even job security.

On their own, many states are investigating the potential for what has been called value-added assessment, which is a term used to mean measuring student growth in achievement from year to year, and for gauging individual teachers' effects on that growth. Of course, accomplishing value-added assessment requires **assessment**—and lots of it. At a minimum, it requires administration of different forms of a standardized test at the beginning and end of each school year, or administration of one form of a test series once each year at the same time. Adding a twist, value-added assessment requires that teachers'

O━━🏛 **Key Idea #3 Exit Examinations**

A 2004 study by the Center for Education Policy found the following:

- As of 2004, 20 states had mandatory high school exit examinations.
- More than half of all public school students (52%) and more than half of all minority public school students (55%) live in states with exit exam requirements.
- Five additional states plan to phase in exit examinations by the year 2009.
- If all states that currently have exit examinations and those that plan to implement them stay on course, roughly 70% of all U.S. public high school students will be affected by such tests by the year 2009.

SOURCE: Center on Education Policy (2004).

impacts on student achievement must be estimated via complex statistical formulations; thus, the potential exists for greatly increased anxiety for students, teachers, and school administrators.

The list continues. We might not often think of classroom testing as **high-stakes**, but in many cases the stakes associated with classroom tests are as high as any. Consider the consequences for a student passing or failing a final examination in American Government class—a course credit that is required in many states for high school graduation. The decision to award or deny a diploma based on classroom performance is as high-stakes as it gets.

Many states and school districts have also recently mandated that students pass an "exit examination" as one hurdle toward being awarded a high school diploma. In fact, these mandates are not merely that a student pass a single exit examination but, more likely, that they pass a series of tests in core subjects such as English language arts, mathematics, writing, and science.

High-stakes testing continues after high school as well. Most postsecondary schools require a test—usually the ACT Assessment or the SAT—for students seeking admission to higher education. Although college and university personnel consider many factors when making admissions decisions (e.g., class rank, rigor of high school coursework, and community and extracurricular activities), a student's score on the ACT or SAT is surely one of the important sources of information considered in admissions and scholarship decisions, making a student's performance on those tests a high-stakes endeavor. Even after a student has been admitted, many colleges and universities require additional testing for placement into courses or programs.

The Graduate Record Examination (GRE), Miller Analogies Test (MAT), Medical College Admissions Test (MCAT), Law School Admissions Test (LSAT), and Graduate Management Admissions Test (GMAT) are just a few examples of high-stakes tests that may be required of students seeking further higher education or entrance into a profession. Even after successful completion of a graduate or professional degree (and all the tests along the way), a student may still be required to pass a board examination in order to enter his or her chosen medical profession, or a licensure or certification test to practice in fields as diverse as engineering, cosmetology, real estate, accounting, and numerous others.

To be sure, many students do not pursue education beyond high school. But that doesn't mean that the testing ends. To enter any branch of the military, young men and women must take the Armed Services Vocational Aptitude Battery (ASVAB). The term **battery** refers to a grouping of several tests, and the ASVAB is an extensive, rigorous, and lengthy test with consequences. For example, different levels of performance are required for entering various branches of the armed services.

Even if a student doesn't plan a military career, he or she will ordinarily need to pass a multiple-choice test consisting of perhaps 20 **items**, as well as a separate performance test just to obtain a driver's license. In fact, now that we think about it, the occasion of obtaining our own driver's licenses was one of the more anxiety-filled testing experiences we can recall. The consequences of failure—limited mobility, restricted access to economic, social, and leisure opportunities, and, not least of all, humiliation within peer group—made this one of the highest-stakes tests of all!

In summary, our consideration of test anxiety is motivated largely by the sheer pervasiveness of testing in American education. Testing has become more extensive and more consequential at every level. The more that important decisions hinge on test results, the more relevant is the concern about the presence and effects of test anxiety. The situation has been summarized by leading researchers on test anxiety. According to Spielberger and Vagg (1995):

> Aptitude and achievement test scores, as well as academic performance, are increasingly used in evaluating applicants for jobs and admission into educational programs. Consequently, examination stress and test anxiety have become pervasive problems in modern society. (p. xiii)

As we conclude this rationale for why thinking about test anxiety is more relevant now than ever before, we are ourselves amazed at the extent of testing and at the important decisions that are increasingly linked to test results. We hope that this overview of testing in American schools and society hasn't induced too much anxiety for our readers. Our goal has simply been to illustrate the ubiquity of testing and to give examples of some of the consequences associated with testing that can instill test anxiety. In the context of the increasing frequency and stakes associated with testing in American schools—particularly the growth of testing associated with the No Child Left Behind Act and related accountability systems—we believe that it is particularly timely to consider the phenomenon of test anxiety, its effects, and how it can be addressed.

A Historical Reminder

Finally, we must admit to something of a contradiction. We have noted that the current context makes concern about test anxiety particularly salient. However, we also must admit that test anxiety and high-stakes testing are not new.

Test anxiety has existed as long as there have been tests. Consider the "examination" administered by the Gilead guards who challenged the fugitives from Ephraim who tried to cross the Jordan River. That event has been described (see Mehrens & Cizek, 2001, p. 477) as one of the earliest-recorded, large-scale, high-stakes performance tests:

> "Are you a member of the tribe of Ephraim?" they asked. If the man replied that he was not, then they demanded, "Say Shibboleth." But if he couldn't pronounce the H and said Sibboleth instead of Shibboleth he was dragged away and killed. So forty-two thousand people of Ephraim died there. (Judges 12:5–6, *The Living Bible*)

We imagine that many of the 42,000 Ephraimites felt a high degree of test anxiety as they stepped forward for their turn to say "Shibboleth." We imagine that a debilitating level of test anxiety was experienced by the poor Ephraimite who was next in line for the test after the Ephraimite in front of him had just been dragged away and killed.

In modern times, testing has become increasingly prominent in schools around the world, but particularly in American schools and society. Entire books on the American culture of testing have been written; one author referred to America, in the title of one such book, as "the credential society" (Collins, 1979). An early researcher on test anxiety commented in the 1950s: "We live in a test-conscious, test-giving culture in which the lives of people are in part determined by their test performance" (Sarason, 1959, p. 26). Going back to the 1930s, a commentator on two student suicides that had occurred at the University of Chicago opined that

> one of these [suicides] was definitely due to worry over an approaching examination and the other presumably was. These incidents show that students are taking their examinations more and more seriously, and that the emotional reactions of students before examinations is an important problem. (Brown, 1938, cited in Spielberger, Gonzalez, Taylor, Algaze, & Anton, 1978, p. 167)

Test Anxiety: Still Hazy After All These Years

We recognize that the high stakes associated with today's educational tests are not nearly as high as those in the Biblical example, and we observe that test anxiety is not a new phenomenon attributable to the rising importance of grades, getting into college, the mandates of No Child Left Behind, or the recent introduction of meaningful educational accountability systems. Nonetheless, the amount and importance of tests used in education has increased. So has the potential for test anxiety.

Unfortunately, just as the potential for and concern about test anxiety has increased, so has the confusion about what test anxiety actually is, what causes it, who is affected, and what can be done about it. There is much misunderstanding about test anxiety.

For example, we note that test anxiety can occur even in situations where there are very low stakes or none at all. On the other hand, many test takers are not affected adversely by test anxiety even when faced with tests that have very serious consequences attached to performance. Another example lies in a popular misunderstanding about test anxiety: Test anxiety is not the normal nervousness we experience in testing situations. That feeling of nervousness is the perfectly normal response that nearly everyone experiences when faced with any challenging task.

In the following chapters, we will provide a more in-depth examination of what test anxiety is. We will try to distinguish it from related but different concepts that often have clouded understanding and created controversy concerning the phenomenon. We will describe how test anxiety can be harmful. And—perhaps to the surprise of some readers—we also will describe how test anxiety can be helpful. We will summarize research findings regarding characteristics of students and settings that are related to test anxiety. Ultimately, we will provide concrete, specific ways that those findings can be translated into positive actions and recommendations for addressing test anxiety and stemming its effects.

Test anxiety may be bad news for many parents, students, and educators. The good news is that there is much that parents, teachers, school systems, and even students themselves can do about it.

2

What Test Anxiety Is . . . and Isn't

"**W**e're having a pop quiz today."

That sentence, uttered by a teacher, had a terrifying effect. In the "old days" referred to in the previous chapter, pop quizzes were fairly common. As students back then, we don't recall ever hearing a teacher explicitly articulate her motive for giving pop quizzes, but we got the main idea: keep current in the readings, homework assignments, and studying. We also got **test anxiety**.

The use of pop quizzes appears to have waned somewhat in today's elementary and secondary school classrooms. Perhaps the decline has been in response to the realization that, in addition to the likely effect on study habits, they also generally tended to increase anxiety about testing. Although the announcement of a pop quiz certainly got our attention, it did not result in debilitating test anxiety for all students, or even most of them. In fact, as we will see later in this chapter, test anxiety affects a surprisingly small percentage of schoolchildren.

That fact, of course, doesn't diminish the reality that test anxiety can pose serious threats to individual students, that it can place the accurate interpretation of test scores at risk, and, ultimately, that it can hinder learning. However, before we look at the incidence of test anxiety and its effects, we will first attempt to define the concept more fully than we did in Chapter 1 and to distinguish it from other, related concepts.

Test Anxiety (and Some Impostors)

Test anxiety is a subcategory of the more general concept, **anxiety**. Anxiety is a phenomenon that has been thoroughly studied and described by psychologists; on a more personal level, it is likely that all of us have personally experienced being anxious at one time or another. However, to say that someone is anxious has a very different meaning to a psychologist than it has to many nonpsychologists. It is not uncommon to hear someone say something like, "I am so anxious to get my new car!" For that person, being anxious translates into a feeling of eager anticipation of a happy event or a good result.

To a psychologist, however, being anxious is not the anticipation of something good. Rather, it is the internal feeling of dread or tension that a person experiences despite the fact that no real, tangible threat to the person exists. Psychologists contrast being anxious with having **fear**. The major distinction is that anxiety is an unrealistic or exaggerated response to a perceived threat, whereas fear is a reasonable, appropriate response to a real threat. Both fear and anxiety can be accompanied by physical, emotional, or cognitive reactions.

Test Anxiety Defined

Test anxiety is considered to be a special form of anxiety, although there remains some lack of conceptual clarity about test anxiety and some uncertainty regarding just how distinct test anxiety is as a characteristic. The concept of test anxiety has been studied in conjunction with other, related concepts such as overanxious disorder (OAD) and social phobia (SP). As it turns out, school-aged children who demonstrate test anxiety also tend to have symptoms of other, more serious disorders. This double whammy is referred to as *comorbidity* in the field of psychiatry. According to one study, "fear of poor performance and negative evaluation by others are common among children with OAD as well as SP" (Beidel, 1991, p. 546).

Because test anxiety is often intertwined with other anxieties and phobias, it is difficult to isolate test anxiety and provide a clear definition of the phenomenon. A number of researchers have attempted to describe test anxiety, but surprisingly few offer straightforward definitions. One source (Zeidner, 1998) provides a comprehensive though rather technical definition. According to Zeidner, test anxiety is the set of phenomenological, physiological, and behavioral responses that accompany concern about possible negative consequences or failure on an exam or similar evaluative situation. . . . Test-anxious students are characterized by a particularly low threshold for anxiety in evaluative situations, tending to view evaluative situations, in general, and test situations in particular as personally threatening. . . . Test-anxious behavior is typically evoked when a person believes that her or his intellectual, motivational, and social capabilities and capacities are taxed or exceeded by demands stemming from the test situation. (pp. 17–18)

In other words, test anxiety is a constellation of responses to **evaluation.** Those responses can be diverse, including physical responses such as rapid breathing, sweating, or racing heart rate. Or the responses can comprise behavioral responses such as pencil tapping, staring, squirming, pacing, fidgeting, or even cheating. Because tests frequently result in the assignment of a grade or score—that is, in an evaluation—test anxiety is experienced in testing situations by persons who feel threatened by evaluation. That threat is most likely to be aroused when a test taker perceives that the evaluation of his or her test performance is likely to be low. That perception arises because the student believes that his or her knowledge, skill, or ability is inadequate to perform successfully on the test.

Interestingly, because whatever level of test anxiety is aroused in a student often depresses his or her test performance, the test taker's perceptions of the threat of evaluation turn out to be accurate, to a degree. That is, the anxiety causes a poor evaluation, which confirms the student's initial perceptions regarding the (un)likelihood of success, which reinforces evaluation as a threatening event.

How Test Anxiety Operates

In the preceding section, we touched on how test anxiety affects students and their test performance, but only in a general way. Many researchers have, however, worked diligently to identify more precisely how test anxiety operates. According to one review of the research on test anxiety, many different possibilities have been examined. For example, some studies have identified the root of test anxiety as lying in students' poor preparation. Those studies suggest that some students ineffectively organize or process information; they perform poorly on tests because of this. Other studies have identified

> O──🔒   **Key Idea #4   How Test Anxiety Operates**
>
> Test anxiety is actually a series of situations, events, and responses that form a continuous cycle.
>
> A student enters an evaluation situation (i.e., a test) with a feeling that the test is a threatening event.
>
> The associated anxiety often lowers the student's test performance.
>
> The poor test performance confirms the student's perceptions of the threat of evaluation.
>
> The student enters the next evaluation situation with a stronger feeling that the test is a threatening event in which he or she is likely to perform poorly.

the "habitual, irrelevant, negative thoughts that some students have during a testing situation" as a major cause of test anxiety (Mealey & Host, 1992, p. 147).

According to Mealey and Host (1992), there are three main categories of test-anxious students. The categories include students who

1. do not have adequate study and test-preparation strategies, realize that deficiency, know they are not well prepared for testing situations, and are worried;

2. have adequate strategies in their repertoire and use them but become distracted during testing; and

3. mistakenly believe they have adequate strategies, do poorly on tests, and anxiously wonder why. (p. 148)

Unfortunately, explaining test anxiety is not as simple as figuring out which category a student belongs in. After more than half a century of research devoted to the topic, a clearer conception of what test anxiety is has begun to emerge. As it turns out, addressing test anxiety requires an understanding of how a fairly complicated process operates. In the following sections, the distinction between two kinds of anxiety is presented. Then, two components of anxiety are described. Finally, using these concepts, a complete model of how we believe test anxiety actually operates is provided and illustrated.

Key Idea #5   Three Different Students With Test Anxiety

The True Perceiver: This student accurately realizes that he or she did not adequately prepare for an upcoming test and/or does not have adequate test-preparation skills. The student is anxious about the upcoming test—with good reason.

The Unfocussed: This student may have mastered the content of an upcoming test and/or may possess adequate test-taking skills. However, the student is easily distracted during testing; as a result, he or she is unable to access knowledge or apply skills and performs poorly.

The Misapprehender: This student inaccurately believes that he or she possesses adequate knowledge and/or test-taking skills. When confronted with poor test performance, the conflicting information causes worry, confusion, and anxiety.

SOURCE: Adapted from Mealey and Host (1992).

Traits and States

To begin understanding test anxiety, it is important to first distinguish between different kinds of anxiety in general. Psychologists make a distinction between what is called *trait anxiety* and *state anxiety*. A **trait** is an enduring characteristic of a person. Trait anxiety is a fairly stable characteristic that has pervasive effects or is evident in diverse aspects of a person's life. People differ in their levels of trait anxiety, and such variation is perfectly normal. People who are high in trait anxiety are generally more anxious across diverse settings and contexts than people who are low in trait anxiety. For such people, the experience of anxiety and perceptions of threatening situations are not limited to a specific event such as a test. It might be helpful to think of people high in trait anxiety as relatively more "high strung" or simply as more anxious in general than others. People low in trait anxiety might be thought of as more "low key" or "laid back" than others. Most people are somewhat in the middle, with a comparatively moderate level of trait anxiety.

In contrast, a **state** is a temporary phenomenon. State anxiety is a form of anxiety that is evident only in specific situations. People differ in terms of state anxiety, but in a somewhat different way than the way in which they differ on trait anxiety. For example, some people

---

> ⊙━🁢   **Key Idea #6   States and Traits**
>
> A **state** is a temporary characteristic or feeling that a person experiences. State anxiety is a kind of anxiety that is evident only in specific situations.
>
> A **trait** is an enduring characteristic of a person. Trait anxiety is a fairly stable characteristic with pervasive effects and/or is evident in diverse aspects of a person's life.

---

experience state anxiety when they fly in an airplane, when they must give a speech in front of a large group, when they visit the dentist, when they are in an enclosed space, and so on. State anxiety is experienced in different specific situations for different people and to differing degrees. An important part of the distinction between trait anxiety and state anxiety is that a person who experiences state anxiety in a specific situation (e.g., when giving a speech) may be either relatively low or high on trait anxiety. In fact, giving a speech might be the only situation in which a person experiences anxiety. However, a person high on trait anxiety is more anxious generally, across a variety of situations. They experience some level of anxiety regularly, and perceive diverse contexts—which may be completely unrelated—to be threatening.

Researchers have found that students who experience test anxiety tend to have higher levels of trait anxiety as a general characteristic of their personalities. That higher level of general (trait) anxiety causes some students to perceive a testing situation as more threatening to begin with than do other students. The specific (state) anxiety prompted by a testing situation for students with greater anxiety levels in the first place results in more serious effects.

Worry and Emotionality

Another important prerequisite for understanding how test anxiety operates is the distinction between the two major components of test anxiety. In the late 1960s, two researchers (Liebert & Morris, 1967) theorized that two elements contributed to test anxiety: worry and emotionality. According to Liebert and Morris, **emotionality** comprises the physiological aspect of test anxiety. That is, it encompasses the

Key Idea #7   Two Components of Test Anxiety

Emotionality is the physical component of test anxiety that is observable in certain physiological responses to a testing situation. The manifestations of emotionality include nervousness, pacing, pencil-tapping, constantly looking at the clock, sweating, fidgeting, and so on.

Worry is the psychological or cognitive component of test anxiety. Worry is evident in a student's preoccupation before and/or during testing with the consequences of poor performance or of failing the test. Students who think or verbalize a negative or pessimistic expectation are manifesting the worry component.

physical reactions or responses to test situations, such as nervousness, sweating, fidgeting, and so on. **Worry**, by contrast, comprises the psychological or cognitive aspect of test anxiety. That is, worry relates primarily to "cognitive concern[s] about the consequences of failure" (p. 975). Students experiencing test anxiety do not approach a task such as a test with a positive outlook or expectation of success, but with dread regarding the potential for negative evaluation or failure. Researchers have isolated the worry component of test anxiety as the culprit primarily responsible for depressing test performance in students with high levels of test anxiety.

Models of Test Anxiety

When researchers speak of models, they are not referring to the plastic, scaled-down replicas of airplanes or cars that hobbyists assemble or to the super variety that demonstrate how to wear the latest fashions. Instead, scientists refer to models as concrete ways of representing abstract or complex systems of relationships. Models are helpful ways of thinking about how what is seen but cannot be directly observed relates to what cannot be seen but is of greatest interest. For example, a student's level of test anxiety is something that cannot be viewed by a teacher or counselor; students' actual levels of test anxiety cannot be directly measured or examined. Rather, what is observed are only the students' outward manifestations of test anxiety, such as the emotionality responses described earlier. In order to attempt to understand test anxiety, psychologists and psychometricians use instruments (ironically, tests) to measure test anxiety indirectly. They use the results of these measurements from things they can actually observe to infer something about those characteristics of interest that cannot be observed. Often, elaborate explanatory frameworks are developed to make the relationship between the observed and the underlying more concrete. These frameworks are called models.

Early researchers in the area of test anxiety postulated rival, alternative models of test anxiety. One perspective on test anxiety was found in what are called the *interference models*. The major characteristic of interference models is the conceptualization that test performance (observed) is depressed because of interference with memory, recall, information processing, and so on. According to the interference models, test anxiety (unobserved) occurs because factors such as worry and emotionality (unobserved) interfere with normal performance.

The other perspective on test anxiety has been captured in what are called *deficit models*. These models suggest that the detrimental effects of test anxiety operate because test takers lack some knowledge or skill that is important for demonstrating his or her true level of ability. For example, in the deficit models, a test taker might lack good study habits, self-efficacy, test-taking skills, and so on.

Current research on test anxiety, however, suggests that neither the interference model nor the deficit model fully captures the complex relationships and factors that underlie test anxiety. A very different and considerably more complex model is now widely accepted as a more accurate framework for thinking about test anxiety.

Two of the leading researchers on test anxiety, Charles Spielberger and Peter Vagg (1995), have synthesized the various aspects of test anxiety into what they have termed a *transactional model* of how the phenomenon occurs. They refer to their model as transactional to highlight that test anxiety is best thought of as a process or cycle of thoughts, behaviors, and responses. Their model is an attempt to bring together background characteristics of students, elements of the testing situation, and what is known about how humans process information, to create a graphical representation of how test anxiety operates. A version of their model appears in Figure 2–1.

According to this model, the process begins when a person is presented with a task (I) such as a test. Immediately, the person forms perceptions (II) related to the task. These perceptions are about the test taker himself or herself (e.g., "This test looks like something I am prepared for" or "I don't think I'm ready for this"). And the perceptions are related to the task at hand (e.g., "These test questions look hard"

Figure 2–1 Transactional Model of Test Anxiety

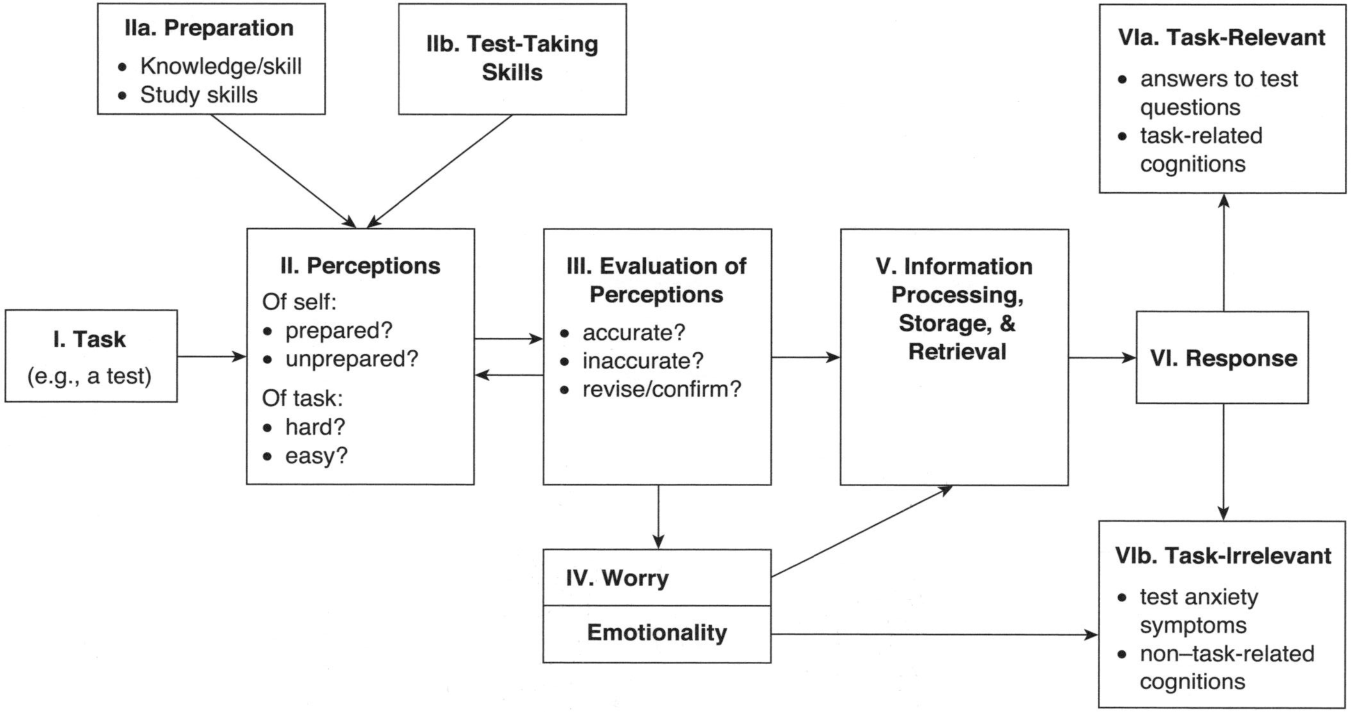

IIa. Preparation
- Knowledge/skill
- Study skills

IIb. Test-Taking Skills

I. Task
(e.g., a test)

II. Perceptions

Of self:
- prepared?
- unprepared?

Of task:
- hard?
- easy?

III. Evaluation of Perceptions
- accurate?
- inaccurate?
- revise/confirm?

IV. Worry

Emotionality

V. Information Processing, Storage, & Retrieval

VI. Response

VIa. Task-Relevant
- answers to test questions
- task-related cognitions

VIb. Task-Irrelevant
- test anxiety symptoms
- non–task-related cognitions

or "This looks easy"). Coming into play to form these perceptions are the student's actual level of preparation, time spent studying, and study skills (IIa), as well as his or her familiarity with the test format and test-taking skills (IIb).

The test taker's perceptions about self and task are then subjected to an internal, subjective evaluation (III). At this internal evaluation stage, the student subconsciously attempts to ascertain how accurate these perceptions are. The evaluation is ongoing and cyclical, as the student constantly forms and reforms perceptions about self and task at hand and appraises the accuracy of those perceptions.

For students with relatively higher levels of trait anxiety, the initial perceptions and appraisals of those perceptions result in a view of the situation as somewhat threatening, with the corresponding increase in emotionality and worry (IV), which in turn interferes with cognitive processes (V) and, ultimately, affects the responses (VI) produced in the testing situation. These responses are usually a mixed bag. One type of response facilitates test performance; these responses are relevant (VIa) to the task at hand (i.e., the test) and they promote an accurate indication of the student's true level of knowledge or skill. Another type of response—task-irrelevant responses (VIb)—can impair test performance and includes the observable symptoms of test anxiety as well as thoughts and ideas that are unproductive or unrelated to successful performance of the task. One researcher has summarized the mix of responses in this way: "Test-anxious persons divide their attention between task-relevant activities and preoccupations with worry, self-criticism, and [physical or bodily] concerns. With less attention available for task-directed efforts, their performance is depressed" (Hembree, 1988, p. 48).

An Illustration of the Transactional Model

To illustrate how this model operates, let us imagine a high school student, Jason, who is about to take an examination in biology class. Jason is a good student: he has attended classes, turned in homework on time, earned Bs and Cs on assignments, and so on. He has only a moderately high level of trait anxiety. Now, suppose that Jason begins the biology test by carefully examining the first question. If the first question appears to him to be difficult and he judges himself to not be adequately prepared for the test, he may have a difficult time choosing the correct response to a multiple-choice item or writing a correct response to an essay question. Because he experiences difficulty in answering the first question, his initial negative perceptions of the task or self are evaluated to be accurate. This evaluation stimulates the reactions of worry and emotionality. Emotionality leads to the symptoms of anxiety mentioned previously (e.g., fidgeting or increased heart rate), which are behaviors that are not relevant to success on the task at hand. And his worrying interferes with his ability to think clearly, to retrieve and process the biology content he has learned. He marks an answer to the first question, though he is unsure if his answer is correct. This leads to an increase in state anxiety—that is, test anxiety—which induces more negative evaluations when Jason begins to examine question number two on the biology test.

Jason's experience with the first question, the resulting increase in worry and emotionality, and the resulting decrease in cognitive and behavioral actions that would help him do his best work on the test combine to confirm his initial appraisal. As he attempts subsequent questions on the test, there is an increased tendency for him to perceive the test to be hard and himself to be unprepared. When all is said and done, things do not go as well for Jason on the biology test as he had hoped.

Jason's experience can be contrasted with that of his classmate, Adrian, who is very similar to Jason. Adrian, too, is a good student and has only a moderately high level of trait anxiety. However, Adrian has learned some test-taking skills to help head off any potentially impairing effects of test anxiety. Adrian skims the test and chooses to answer question number seven first. He evaluates this question to be easy and judges that he is well prepared to answer it. He staves off an increase in worry and emotionality, his ability to recall and process information remains high, he avoids the grip of test anxiety at least temporarily, and he chooses an answer to question seven that he has high confidence is correct. He then proceeds to attempt another question in the test. Adrian is at somewhat of an advantage as he attempts the subsequent question, however. His experience with the previous question has resulted in an increased tendency for him to perceive the test to be manageable and himself to be prepared, and he has not experienced any increased test anxiety. When the test results are returned, Adrian's grade of A– is slightly better than Jason's grade of B+.

These hypothetical scenarios illustrate how test anxiety can operate. In the second scenario, Adrian took advantage of some techniques for tempering the potentially harmful effects of test anxiety. In a subsequent chapter of this book, we will explore many techniques that students, teachers, and parents can use to address test anxiety. However, in the next section of this chapter we examine one myth about test anxiety; namely, that its effects are always harmful. As it turns out, test anxiety is often a very good thing.

**Key Idea #8   Test Anxiety:
A Transactional Phenomenon**

Current thinking about test anxiety suggests that it occurs as a cyclical or recursive process involving students' thoughts, behaviors, and responses. It follows a predictable series of steps:

1. The cycle starts when a student is confronted with a test.

2. The student forms perceptions about the test, his or her test-taking skills, etc.

3. The student subjectively thinks about and evaluates the accuracy of his or her perceptions.

4. For some students, the initial perceptions and evaluations result in a view of the test as a threatening situation. This increases worry and emotionality.

5. Worry and emotionality negatively affect the student's cognitive processing.

6. The negative impact of worry and emotionality affect the student's responses to test questions and ability to perform.

7. Poor test performance affects the student's self-perceptions, which are evoked again (Step II) when the student is next presented with a test (Step I).

Test Anxiety: Sometimes a Good Thing?

A common misconception about test anxiety is that it is uniformly a bad thing. Many reports on test anxiety describe how it depresses test performance, induces insecurity and confusion in otherwise competent students, promotes cheating, and causes crying, fainting, trembling, vomiting, and blurred vision in young children.

But these undesirable effects are actually only half of the story. In 1908, two psychologists, Robert Yerkes and John Dodson, made a number of interesting discoveries about the relationship between anxiety (they called it "arousal") and performance. To begin with, they were the first to document that, in most cases, there is not a direct relationship between anxiety and performance. That is, increasing anxiety does not always lead to decreased performance. In fact, Yerkes and Dodson (1908) were the first to demonstrate the now well-accepted notion of a curvilinear or inverted, U-shaped relationship, which is illustrated in Figure 2–2.

Figure 2–2   Illustration of "Facilitative Effect" of Test Anxiety

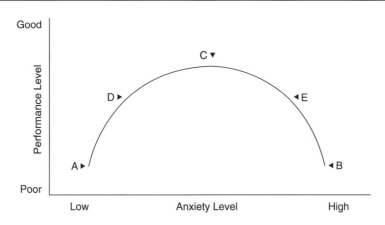

The figure shows a graph on which are plotted two variables, anxiety and performance. The resulting curved line shows the relationship between those variables. Overall, interpretation of the graph is straightforward, but three positions along the curve are marked for further explanation.

First, let us consider a person for whom position A on the graph is an accurate description. This person has nearly the lowest level of anxiety (or arousal) imaginable. Such a person might be thought of as "flat" or completely unmotivated. In a sports-related context, an athlete at position A might be described as not "psyched up" or not "up for the game." In school-related situations, such a person would appear to be unconcerned about an upcoming test—perhaps so unworried as to not even bother preparing for it. The graph shows the (usual) corresponding performance of such a person. In athletic competitions, a coach will often explain that his or her team lost the game because the players were down or flat or not up for the game. In academic situations, a low level of arousal often portends failure as well.

Now let us consider a person for whom position B on the graph is an accurate description. This person has nearly the highest level of anxiety or arousal imaginable. Such a person might be thought of as "stoked" or "wired." In a sports-related context, an athlete at position A might be described as "pumped" or "strung tight." In school-related situations, such a person would appear to be immensely concerned about an upcoming test—perhaps so worried that it has become their sole focus. In this case, the graph also shows the (usual) corresponding performance of such a person. In athletic contests, competitors with overly high levels of anxiety often perform poorly; we call this "choking." In education contexts, similar overly high levels of anxiety can result in choking in test situations.

Finally, let us consider a person a person for whom position C on the graph is an accurate description. This person has a moderate level of anxiety. If we extended the sports analogy, such a person would be "fired up" or "have their game face on." In schools, we might think of such a person as concerned or as a little nervous about the test. In any event, the graph shows the usual—and beneficial—performance level that corresponds to that level of anxiety. As the graph indicates, it is the person with a moderate level of anxiety that has the highest level of performance.

The phenomenon described by Yerkes and Dodson (1908) has come to be called the "facilitative effect" of anxiety. That is, some anxiety actually facilitates improved performance. And educators can take advantage of this principle. For example, let us imagine a student at position D on the graph. For this student, adding some measure of concern, arousal, or anxiety regarding the test would actually likely improve his or her performance. However, if we imagined a student at position E on the graph, we might want to implement some strategies to lessen the concern or anxiety he or she was experiencing regarding an upcoming test, to help him or her display optimal performance.

The work of Yerkes and Dodson (1908) has led to a second important implication. As we have come to fully understand their principle regarding the relationship between anxiety and performance, we have also learned that it is not always as simple as the inverted U-shaped diagram might suggest. For example, we now know that there is an interaction between the level of arousal or anxiety required for the best performance on a task and the difficulty of the task itself. As a general rule, it appears that a moderate level of anxiety is appropriate for eliciting a student's best performance on a test when the test is of moderate difficulty. This is just what the graph predicts. However, a relatively higher level of anxiety is necessary for best performance when the task is perceived to be very easy, and a relatively lower level of anxiety is preferred when the task is perceived to be very difficult.

Many educators might recognize this slight modification of Yerkes and Dodson's (1908) principle as part of the folk wisdom of teaching that has found its way into the very organization of schools. The principle can be recognized in the fact that many schools schedule various subjects according to their perceived difficulty and the commonly accepted notions of how arousal levels change over the course of the day. For example, it is widely believed that arousal tends to increase over the course of the day. Thus, it would make sense to schedule those tasks that students would perceive to be most difficult or challenging for the morning hours, when arousal is at its lowest level. Conversely, following the implication of Yerkes and Dodson's principle, it would make sense to schedule easier or less-challenging tasks later in the day. Thus, we can now recognize why it is common practice, particularly in the elementary grades, for schools to teach "harder" subjects such as reading or mathematics early in the school day and to teach "easier" subjects like physical education or art in the afternoon. This explains, too, why important tests—like state-mandated proficiency tests—are also often scheduled for the first part of a school day.

Summary

In this chapter, we have tried to clear up a number of misconceptions about test anxiety and to clarify the concept before we proceed any further. Test anxiety is not the normal nervousness that most everyone experiences before or during taking a test. A test is an evaluation of a person's skill or ability. We often take these evaluations personally and want to be seen in our best light when we are evaluated for any reason. When taking a test, it is natural to experience some anxiety at the prospect of personal evaluation. It would be more abnormal if we *didn't* become more anxious under test circumstances or under other circumstances when we must perform—especially when there are consequences associated with successful or unsuccessful performance.

Test anxiety is not simply a matter of a person becoming extraordinarily nervous under such circumstances, either. A number of factors come into play in creating and sustaining test anxiety. The model of how test anxiety operates, presented earlier in this chapter, portrays the complex mechanisms—as we currently understand them—that play a part in test anxiety and that help explain why people differ in their levels of that characteristic.

These conclusions imply the next steps in our look at test anxiety. First, the notion that test anxiety is a characteristic on which people differ suggests that it might be helpful to understand those differences. One way to do so is to try to measure the different levels of test anxiety that students possess. In Chapter 5, we provide a brief introduction to measuring test anxiety. Examples of some instruments useful for measuring test anxiety are reproduced in Appendix C.

Second, the fact that the presence of a large amount of test anxiety can be detrimental to performance is an obvious concern for educators. It is clear that strategies for reducing test anxiety—and thereby its effects—would be beneficial for many students. Methods that can be used by teachers, parents, and students themselves are presented in Chapter 6.

Finally, although we know that test anxiety can be detrimental, it seems important to first understand just how pervasive test anxiety really is. And the observation that people differ in their levels of test anxiety suggests that it is also important to understand the factors that relate to higher or lower levels of that characteristic. These topics are the focus of our next chapter.

3

The Effects of Test Anxiety on Students and Teachers

The purpose of this chapter is to put test anxiety into context—actually, into multiple contexts. One way to put test anxiety into context is to answer the important question, what are the effects of test anxiety? We might view test anxiety differently if its effects were mild rather than severe. To answer this question, we present information on how test anxiety affects students, teachers, and test scores.

Of course, even once the effects of test anxiety are known, it is reasonable to ask, How prevalent is test anxiety? We might have a different level of concern about test anxiety—even if its effects were quite serious—depending on whether it affects very many or very few test takers. We begin this chapter with an attempt to ascertain how common test anxiety actually is.

How Much of a Problem Is Test Anxiety?

It has been estimated that the field of test anxiety research is approximately 50 years old. It would be reasonable to assume that after a half century of study we would have a fairly good idea about the prevalence of test anxiety. Such an assumption would, however, be incorrect. Consider the following estimates of the prevalence of test anxiety offered by leading researchers in the field:

- Between 25% and 30% of American students suffer effects of debilitating stress in evaluative situations (Hill, 1984).
- Between 34% and 41% of third- through sixth-grade children are affected by test anxiety (Turner, Beidel, Hughes, & Turner, 1993).
- Test anxiety . . . is a common, treatable condition that may lower student performance in up to 10% of the school-aged population (Erford & Moore-Thomas, 2004).
- Approximately 20% of students (i.e., approximately one out of five) in upper elementary school are hindered in demonstrating their ability because of test anxiety (Goonan, 2004).
- About two or three children in a typical classroom are highly anxious. . . . As many as 10 million students in elementary and secondary school [are] performing poorer on tests than they should because anxiety and deficiencies in test-taking strategies interfere with their performance (Wigfield & Eccles, 1989).
- Approximately 1.1% of school-aged children worry about making mistakes (Beidel, 1991).

For many reasons, it is difficult to make any sense of these estimates. First, we might notice the great variability in the figures cited. The lower estimates would mean that we would expect only 1 or 2 children in a typical classroom of, say, 20 to 25 children to be affected by test anxiety. The midrange estimate of 20% would translate into 4 or 5 students. The high-end estimate of 40% would mean that 8 to 10 students were affected. The wide variety of the estimates—ranging from almost no students affected to nearly half of them—means that we simply don't currently know enough about the prevalence of test anxiety.

Second, it is difficult to interpret these figures because researchers tend to use different definitions of what they are estimating—not necessarily confining themselves to strictly parallel definitions of test anxiety. For example, the 1.1% estimate refers to the percentage of students who worry about making mistakes. The 10% estimate refers to the percentage of elementary school children who are highly anxious. The 20% estimate represents the percentage of children who are hindered from showing their real ability on tests, and it includes poor performance because of either test anxiety or poor test-taking skills. The 25% to 30% figure is an estimate of the percentage of children who suffer from debilitating stress. The highest estimate (41%) refers to the percentage of students who are generally affected by test anxiety.

Finally, estimates of the prevalence of test anxiety have used different methods, have examined different samples of students at different grade levels, and have been collected at different times. It is reasonable to conclude that actual levels of test anxiety differ across grade levels and differ according to the amount and importance of testing in any given year or any particular state or school district.

We are not critical of what researchers have discovered, but we are eager to see better information generated by more study of test anxiety in the future. Clearly, researchers have attempted to obtain precise quantitative estimates of the prevalence of test anxiety. However, just as clearly, it is uncertain what the resulting numbers actually mean. It is no wonder that, despite the available information, one leading authority on test anxiety concludes that "data on the prevalence and incidence of test anxiety are surprisingly sparse" (Zeidner, 1998, p. 6).

What Are the Effects of Test Anxiety?

Although the data on the prevalence of test anxiety are sparse, what data are available suggest that test anxiety affects a substantial enough percentage of students that it should be taken seriously. When the hard data is combined with anecdotal teacher reports of the effects of test anxiety on children and adolescents, the problem of test anxiety can be seen in terms of the lives of real students. In the following sections, we describe some of the effects of test anxiety—effects that many educators and other readers of this book are likely to have witnessed firsthand. First, we look directly at the effects of

---

O━🗝━   Key Idea #9   Prevalence of Test Anxiety

Current estimates of the percentage of students in a classroom affected by test anxiety range from a low of about 1% to a high of over 40%.

Using midrange estimates and an average class size of 25, the number of students affected by test anxiety in a given classroom is probably in the range of 4 or 5 students.

More research, using common definitions of test anxiety and better methods for measuring it, is needed to get a more precise idea of the real prevalence of test anxiety.

test anxiety on test takers; that is, on students. Next, we examine the effects of test anxiety on test givers—that is, on teachers, counselors, and other educators, who administer tests ranging from typical informal classroom tests to larger-scale formal examinations, such as statewide student proficiency tests or tests used as part of the process for making important postsecondary decisions (e.g., SAT or ACT). Finally, we explore the effect of test anxiety on the results of tests— that is, on test scores.

Effects on Students

It is no surprise to any teacher to read that students are affected by testing and test anxiety. What may be mildly surprising, however, is to read that there are both negative and positive effects.

To the extent that concerns about doing well, getting good grades, and so on compel students to work harder, to learn certain content or skills, and to become somewhat nervous about an upcoming test over that material, this comparatively mild form of anxiety might be considered a positive effect. In fact, in one recent study (Mass Insight Education, 2002), 140 randomly selected urban high school students were interviewed to determine their perceptions about the high-stakes high school graduation test in place for students in Massachusetts. The survey of student opinions about the Massachusetts Comprehensive Assessment System (MCAS) revealed that

- 67% of students who failed the MCAS the first time they took it said that, as a result, they are working harder in school (p. 4); 65% said that they pay more attention in class since failing the MCAS (p. 5);
- 74% reported that they consider themselves to be more able in math, reading or writing because they have to pass the MCAS in order to graduate (p. 5); and
- 53% said that they get more help and attention from teachers since getting their MCAS results (p. 5).

There are many other positive consequences of testing and of the anxiety that can accompany it (see Cizek, 2001b). For example, to the extent that test results are used for appropriate class placement, to determine appropriate instructional interventions, or to identify the special needs of children, any anxiety accompanying those tests would likely have a positive effect in the long run for students whose educational experiences are enhanced as a result. When interviewed, some students have commented that they actually enjoy the time periods during a school year when testing occurs because they have less homework and less instruction in class (Mulvenon, Stegman, & Ritter, 2003).

Overwhelmingly, however, teachers are more likely to observe and report more negative effects than positive effects of testing on students (O'Sullivan, 1989). Some of the effects are more obvious, more observable, and more serious, such as when a young child cries or becomes ill. Other effects include inappropriate behavior—that is, cheating—which can be motivated by the anxiety associated with testing, evaluation, and grading (see Cizek, 2001a, 2003a).

But there also are more subtle test-anxiety effects that have long-term implications for students. These include the effects of test anxiety on academic motivation, on the attitude of the student toward education, and on the student's self-perceptions of competence as a person or as a learner. Table 3–1 presents an overview of general effects of test anxiety on students.

Table 3–1   General Effects of Test Anxiety on Students

Effect	Relationship(s)
Stress	Test anxiety can induce symptoms of stress, such as crying, acting out, verbalizations
Attitude toward tests and testing	Test anxiety can diminish effort or increase student apathy towards testing
Attitude towards self	Test anxiety can reinforce, induce poor self esteem or poor/inaccurate self-evaluation ("I can't do anything," "I am so stupid . . . ")
Test behavior	Test anxiety can prompt cheating (e.g., sharing or copying of answers, obtaining/using illegal copies of "secure" materials, etc.)
Academic motivation	Test anxiety can decreased student motivation to learn in general
Motivation (future)	Test anxiety can be associated with dropping out of school, grade retention, graduation, placement in special programs/classes
Test anxiety	Effects of test anxiety can "cycle back" to result in successive poor test performance, leading to increased levels of test anxiety

Stress

One of the effects listed in Table 3–1 is stress. Many of us—whether as educators or as students ourselves—have seen, heard of, or experienced the stressful effects of tests. The level of stress experienced can be as mild and unobservable as butterflies in the stomach or can be more visible and serious, like crying. Researchers on the stress effects of testing have investigated the topic in students as young as kindergarten age. In one study, researchers examined kindergartner's stress-related behaviors associated with an achievement test; they observed that children exhibited significantly more stress behaviors during the test than before testing (Fleege, Charlesworth, Burts, & Hart, 1992). The identified stress behaviors included actions like wiggling or squirming in a chair, chewing on pencils, twisting hair, playing with clothes, and complaining of being tired. Other researchers have reported that young student often cry as they become frustrated during a test (Donegan & Trepanier-Street, 1998; Fleege et al., 1992; Gilman & Reynolds, 1991). Sudden student illnesses and students having problems sleeping the night before a test have also been reported.

Interestingly, when parents' and teachers' responses to questions about student-exhibited symptoms of stress are compared, there is some disagreement. In a recent study of elementary school students (Donegan & Trepanier-Street, 1998), parents and teachers responded to a survey that asked whether their children/students exhibited symptoms of stress attributable to testing. As shown in Table 3–2, more teachers than parents reported observing symptoms of stress. The same study collected data on the symptoms that were reported by teachers and parents (Table 3–3), and found that crying was the most frequently reported symptom. Although more teachers than parents participated, the results indicate that parents do not see their children as strongly affected by tests, whereas teachers do. Other

Table 3–2   Teacher and Parent Reports of Frequency of Child Stress Related to Testing

Observed by:	*Reported Frequency of Observation of Student Stress (%)*			
	Never	*Once*	*Occasionally*	*Frequently*
Teacher	15%	5%	63%	17%
Parent	52%	7%	28%	1%

SOURCE: Adapted from Donegan & Trepanier-Street (1998)

Table 3–3 Frequency and Percentage of Symptoms of Student Stress Reported by Teachers and Parents

	Source of Report			
Symptom	Teachers		Parents	
Eating disturbance	8	(5%)	4	(3%)
Sleep disturbance	26	(16%)	8	(6%)
Toileting accidents	5	(3%)	0	(0%)
Crying	42	(26%)	10	(7%)
Illness	34	(21%)	4	(3%)
Resistance to attending school	25	(16%)	8	(6%)
Acting out	35	(22%)	6	(4%)
Withdrawal (at home)	5	(3%)	0	(0%)
Withdrawal (at school)	16	(10%)	4	(3%)
Verbal expressions of concern	97	(61%)	46	(34%)
Other	14	(9%)	6	(4%)

SOURCE: Adapted from Donegan and Trepanier-Street (1998)

 Key Idea #10   Leading Symptoms of Student Test Anxiety

Crying

Not wanting to go to school

Illness

Statements of fear or concern

Difficulty sleeping

Acting out

---

studies have confirmed that parents are not overly concerned about the testing climate at their children's schools, and they generally reject the notion that testing is an overly stressful event (Mulvenon et al., 2003).

Attitude

Testing and test anxiety can have effects on students' attitudes in two areas: (a) in their attitudes toward tests and testing, and (b) in their attitudes toward themselves (e.g., self-concept or self-esteem). The following paragraphs describe these effects, beginning with attitudes toward tests and testing.

It probably comes as no surprise to many teachers that test anxiety can contribute to negative attitudes toward tests and testing. Though it is not as evident in the elementary grades, negative attitudes, avoidance, resistance, and rejection of testing can be routinely observed in test-anxious students in later grades.

Test-anxiety levels have also been shown to relate to self-esteem. Hembree (1988) documented the strong inverse relationship between self-esteem and test anxiety. That is, students with lower self-esteem tend to have higher levels of test anxiety; students with higher self-esteem tend to have lower levels of test anxiety. Other researchers also have found that moderately and highly test-anxious students tend to have poor self-esteem, more negative self-evaluation, and less positive peer relationships than less test-anxious students (Turner et al., 1993).

Inappropriate Testing Behavior

Testing and test anxiety can compel some students to act in inappropriate ways or, to eschew euphemisms, to cheat. Cheating can range from giving an answer to a friend in need to copying an answer from an unwitting classmate to using impermissible resources (e.g., cheat sheets or cell phones) during a test. In fact, the variety of ways that students can cheat is seemingly limitless. Cizek (1999) provides a catalog of methods that test takers use across the primary, secondary, and postsecondary grades. Cizek and other researchers on the topic of cheating have found that the most consistent rationales students offer for such (mis)behavior are anxiety about grades, and competitive pressures for scholarships, class ranking, admission to selective universities, and so on.

Motivation

When looking at the effects of test anxiety on students' motivation, two types of motivation should be considered: (a) the effect on overall academic motivation, and (b) the effect on motivation during tests that may carry future consequences (such as a high school graduation test). As Hill and Wigfield (1984) point out, "Test anxiety is one of the most important aspects of negative motivation and has direct debilitating effects on school performance" (p. 106). In other words, the effect of test anxiety goes beyond just a bad test score.

A student's motivation to learn and a student's approach to school can be greatly affected by test anxiety. Highly anxious students are more sensitive and reactive to evaluation from adults and develop an increased fear of failure. Therefore, anxious students choose tasks that are easier and for which success is more certain. This behavior is referred to as a performance goal orientation, in contrast to students who have a learning goal orientation. Motivational research indicates that performance goal orientation is "ineffective in producing stable confidence, challenge seeking and persistence" (Dweck, 1986, p. 1046). In plain English, this research finding means that real learning–that is, learning that persists through both easy and hard tasks—is more likely to occur when a student is focused on understanding, rather than exclusively on performance as measured by test scores, grade point average (GPA), and so on.

Test anxiety also can affect student motivation on high-stakes tests. Some school administrators feel that test anxiety and bad test experiences can add to the negative experiences that increase the chances that a student will drop out of school (Gilman & Reynolds, 1991). Of course, as we have pointed out previously (and will continue to do throughout this book), many educational phenomena that appear to be simple on the surface are, in reality, considerably more complicated. This applies, too, to the phenomena of dropping out and high-stakes testing.

Dropout Rates

We indicated at the beginning of this section that the effects of test anxiety may be positive or negative, or both. The relationship of test anxiety to dropout rates is best categorized, however, as inconclusive.

The relationship has most often been studied in the context of the exit examinations or graduation tests in specified subject areas that many states require high school seniors to pass to obtain a diploma. The conventional wisdom is generally that such exit examinations tend to increase the frequency of dropping out. In reality, the relationship is—as we hope readers have come to expect—somewhat more complicated.

Obviously, many students do in fact drop out because they are unable to pass such exit examinations, because the anxiety caused by the testing is debilitating, because some students lack motivation to persist, or for other reasons. However, as it turns out, recent research on this relationship reveals that there actually is no net positive or negative effect on dropping out in states that require an exit examination to graduate.

How can this be? A recent study by Greene and Winters (2004) provides some possible explanations. According to the authors:

> [Our] analyses show that implementing a high school exit exam has no significant effect on a state's graduation rate. The results of our analysis might seem counterintuitive to some. . . . Critics may point to the large number of media stories about individual students who cannot pass state tests as proof that testing stops students from graduating. However, while it is certainly the case that exit exams stop at least some students from earning a diploma, there are reasons we might expect them to have no net effect on graduation rates.

> [First], the number of students who fail to graduate because they cannot pass exit exams might be very small. One reason this is plausible is that passing exit exams might require very low levels of proficiency.

> [Second], students have several chances to pass the exams before they are finally denied a diploma. Most students who are serious about graduating high school should be able to pass such an exam if given enough tries, even if only by chance. Also, states that adopt exit exams typically go out of their way to provide extra instruction to students who have failed the test. Thus exit exam requirements may not only be a low hurdle, but students have multiple chances to jump the hurdle.

> [Third], even this small pool of students who cannot pass the exit exam may be canceled out by a similar number of students who do graduate when they otherwise wouldn't have because the test provided schools with an incentive to improve. One idea behind exit exams is that schools . . . will improve the quality of instruction they provide. [Overall], if the number of students positively affected by the adoption of an exit exam is similar to the number of students who cannot pass the test, we would find no relationship between exit exams and graduation rates. (pp. 5–6)

Thus, in addition to motivation factors that prompt negative outcomes such as dropping out, there are motivation factors that contribute to positive outcomes, such as learning, persistence, and eventually earning a high school diploma when a student otherwise may not have. Similar mixed effects of motivation can be seen in the positive and negative effects associated with grade promotion/ retention tests and with exams that affect eligibility for special services or placement in certain programs or classes. In summary, it is simply not possible to conclude that increases in dropout rates can be attributed to the imposition of testing requirements or to the effects of test anxiety.

Effort

At the elementary school level, the relationship between testing, anxiety, and motivation are often less noticeable, and the effects of test anxiety are often less dramatic than dropping out. Elementary school teachers can affirm that young children will, in general, take any test seriously—regardless of the stakes—if told to do so by their teacher. And they generally will regard such tests as important and will expend effort to perform appropriately. As students progress through school, however, their motivation to do well on tests—particularly on tests external to the classroom—appears to decrease. As many high school teachers can affirm, it can be a daunting task to convince students to expend optimum effort on a test that they do not view as particularly relevant.

This age-related behavior is a considerable source of concern for those who develop tests. One context in which this difference can be particularly vexing is in what is called **field testing**. Field testing involves large-scale tryouts of test items, under circumstances in which performance on the items does not "count" for students but only aids the test makers in determining whether the items are of sufficiently high quality to be used on a test that does count. In contexts such as state-mandated testing, field testing often relies on voluntary school district participation. When test makers are developing a test for an elementary grade level, the use of volunteers does not appear to decrease the accuracy of the information yielded by the field tests. For example, if results show that approximately 75% of second-grade students answer a particular comprehension question correctly on a field test, the test maker can be fairly certain that approximately 75% of students will answer the same question correctly when the question appears on the state's official reading test. The younger students tend to approach both tasks with the same generally positive attitude and effort.

The situation is markedly different by the time students reach high school. As some researchers have found, "instead of increasing motivation and testwiseness with age, older students apparently feel greater resentment, anxiety, cynicism and mistrust of standardized achievement tests [and] growing suspicion about the validity of test scores" (Paris, Lawton, Turner, & Roth, 1991, p. 16). As a consequence, many older students feel that tests are a waste of time and do not put forth their best effort, or they may respond by bubbling in patterns on answer sheets or spelling out words on score sheets. The authors of this book have observed these phenomena in state assessment programs, with the effect of such behavior affecting the field-test estimates of item difficulty by as much as 15%. In other words, an item answered correctly by 75% of high school students under nonmotivated field-test conditions might be answered correctly by 90% of students under motivated conditions!

Students who understand that a field test does not count and whose test performance contributes to the phenomenon just described probably have a very low level of test anxiety. They may be unconcerned about how randomly answering questions on a field test affects them, their school, the state's testing program, and so on. However, it is possible that test anxiety is heightened for some students when, as in field testing, the consequences of test performance are unknown or the purpose of the test is vague. For these students who lack the confidence to game the system, such testing might reinforce negative attitudes toward testing, decrease motivation to perform well, and contribute to subsequent heightened test anxiety.

Test Anxiety

Finally, as was implied at the end of the previous section, it must be said that one effect of test anxiety can be to create more test anxiety. In the transactional model of test anxiety described in Chapter 2, it is clear that levels of test anxiety may be elevated by successive poor test performances. The cumulative effects of test anxiety can become more salient and more pronounced as students progress through the educational system and encounter more testing experiences.

Effects on Teachers

Students are not the only ones who experience the effects of testing and test anxiety. Perhaps even more present—yet not as visible—are the effects of testing on teachers. In this section, we are not talking about the direct manifestations of test anxiety in teachers. Though teachers certainly take tests themselves (e.g., for licensure or certification) and

Key Idea #11   Test Anxiety Can Affect Students By

increasing their levels of stress;

causing or reinforcing negative attitudes toward self, subject area, schooling, or testing;

prompting them to cheat on tests;

decreasing levels of motivation;

depressing levels of test performance; and

contributing to greater levels of test anxiety in subsequent testing contexts.

may experience traditional test anxiety in those contexts, in this section, we focus on secondhand test anxiety, or the indirect effects of anxiety when a teacher's students take high-stakes tests. In such situations, teachers (and other affected educators) may not be the test takers, but because the students' test results increasingly figure into accountability and personnel evaluation systems, the fear and emotionality associated with such testing is certainly real.

Some of the effects of test anxiety on teachers and students—stress, pressure, attitude, motivation, and inappropriate test behavior—are quite similar. However, a key difference is the effect of testing and test anxiety on the classroom, on what is taught and on how it is taught. It also appears that the effect of testing on teachers varies across grade levels. Table 3–4 gives an overview of these effects, and we elaborate on the elements of the table in the following sections.

Systemic Stressors

Teachers frequently report that they feel pressure from both school administrators and parents to produce high test scores, and such reports have been well documented (see, e.g., Fleege et al., 1992; Gilman & Reynolds, 1991; Pedulla et al., 2003). One study by Monsaas and Engelhard (1994) surveyed teachers in Georgia, across all grade levels ($n = 96$ elementary; $n = 57$ middle and school junior high; $n = 33$ high school), about systemic pressures to increase test scores. They found not only that the amount of pressure reported by teachers was significant, but also that when a teacher felt a high level of pressure he or she tended to spend more class time on test-preparation activities, compared to teachers who perceived lower levels of pressure.

Table 3–4   General Effects of Test Anxiety on Teachers

Effect	Source/Manifestation
Systemic stress	Pressure from administrators and parents; demands for higher test scores
Personal stress	Personal worry about student performance, professional standing
Morale (low)	Public dissemination/comparison of test scores; blame
Test behavior (inappropriate)	Altering students' answer sheets; allowing extended time on a timed test or inappropriate deviations from standard administration conditions; giving hints to students
Classroom and teaching methods	Teaching to the test (i.e., narrowing of curriculum to only cover what is on the test)

One of the authors of this book (SSB) observed, firsthand, a manifestation of this pressure while visiting a classroom in which a teacher told her class that they had to do well on an approaching standardized test "so that the principal won't fire me." The other author of this book (GJC) received a sobering, anonymous e-mail just prior to completing this manuscript. The writer of the e-mail apparently was aware of the author's previous work in the area of cheating on tests and wanted to communicate the extent and seriousness of the problem. According to the writer:

> Cheating is so unfair to our children. I work at a school where cheating is going on by the Principal, Vice President of the union and the Coordinator in charge of testing. These educators pressure the classroom teachers to cheat. They even coach the teachers how to cheat. This school has the highest test scores in the whole district. The teachers that are forced to cheat are sick and tired of cheating, and scared, but they are afraid if they don't cheat the Principal will make their lives unbearable. One of the teachers told the Principal on the last day that she had found another district to work for and he yelled at her for not letting him know that she was planning to leave. I think he was more concerned that she was going to

break the cheating team. She was afraid of losing her teaching license and tired of cheating, so she decided to save her career and move on. I hate what they are doing to our children of tomorrow. I want this to end. I had plans to report the cheating to the Superintendent, but I was told that she is aware of it. My question is, "How do you stop cheating in your school when the top people are allowing it?"

As this note makes painfully clear, the pressure associated with testing affects school administrators in much the same way as it affects teachers. Moreover, in addition to what might be thought of as negative pressures, many states now offer educators merit pay or bonuses based on student test performance—creating a kind of positive pressure on those who work to earn such bonuses and an additional source of negative pressure on those who fail to do so. At the local level, the systemic source of pressure may also include a board of education. Thus, administrative pressures are often passed down the line to the teachers.

It is likely that the pressure chain is ultimately rooted in public expectations, whether these expectations are expressed informally to local teachers, principals, or school boards or they are expressed more formally in the form of public policy or law. A recent survey of teachers found that over half of the surveyed teachers, regardless of school type (elementary, middle, or high school), agreed with a statement that "they feel pressure from parents to raise scores on the state test" (Pedulla et al., 2003, p. 33).

It is important to note in closing that the stresses of testing do not result in all or even most educators succumbing to the pressure by cheating. It is clear that the vast majority of educators conducts testing in an honest, ethical, and professional way. And, as we have seen previously, some anxiety about performance—in this case, the anxiety experienced by educators who are at least partially responsible for improving student achievement—may be a facilitative force. Nonetheless, the negative effects of such pressures are equally clear.

Morale

The morale of teachers (and other educators) can be adversely affected when test scores are used as a measure of a teacher's effectiveness. Many teachers are opposed to using test scores to compare teachers, schools, and districts. One researcher reports that the publication of test scores produces feelings of shame, embarrassment, guilt, and anger (Smith, 1991). In a recent survey, about 75% of teachers who responded agreed that "the benefits of the testing program are not worth the time and money involved" (Pedulla et al., 2003). As a consequence of the testing required by state accountability systems and federal legislation, some teachers are suffering from lowered morale or increased discontent with the teaching profession, and some are leaving the profession entirely. Those who remain in the profession find ways to sustain morale despite additional professional pressures; some do so by seeking teaching assignments outside of tested grades or subjects.

Personal Stress

Testing can create personal stress for teachers. One study (Mulvenon et al., 2003) reports that over 90% of teachers said they feel at least somewhat anxious about their students' performance on mandated tests. The experience of personal stress is uneven across grade levels. Teachers in the later elementary school grades tend to experience more stress associated with testing than do teachers in either early elementary or high school grades (see Table 3–5).

At least one explanation for this pattern might be that usually more testing is done during early elementary school. Testing in these early grades comprises achievement testing, placement tests, diagnostic examinations, and other assessments that have consequences for students or teachers. Another explanation may be that upper-level teachers can, to a greater degree than can earlier elementary teachers, justify weak student performance as attributable to previous, ineffective instruction. Finally, an additional source of stress for early elementary teachers may be related to the feelings of guilt and anxiety they often experience when administering mandated tests to

Table 3–5   Percentage of Teachers Reporting Incidences of Personal Stress Related to Testing

	Reported Incidence		
Grade Range	*Never*	*Occasionally*	*Frequently/Consistently*
Lower Elementary	27.1%	31.3%	41.7%
Upper Elementary	3.7%	42.6%	52.7%

SOURCE: Adapted from Donegan & Trepanier-Street (1998).

young children, because many early educators view such testing as developmentally inappropriate.

Inappropriate Testing Behaviors

Another effect of testing-related anxiety is that it can compel inappropriate test behavior; that is, cheating. Not only test takers but also test givers (i.e., teachers) sometimes cheat, and anxiety about accountability pressures is likely the major factor in educator cheating. The most blatant form of cheating would be to steal, reproduce, and teach students the questions covered by a secure test form. This happens, but it is likely not the most common type of cheating. Other inappropriate behaviors include providing impermissible help to students during a structured test, such as allowing extended time when the allotted amount is up, giving hints on answer selections, or using secure copies of tests for review or practice.

In one recent example of the subtle ways that cheating can occur, the principal of a Florida elementary school was accused of trying to manipulate the school's performance on the Florida Comprehensive Assessment Test (FCAT). According to a newspaper report, the principal allegedly wrote a memo to her staff, asking them to list students who were frequently tardy, absent, late being picked up from school, suffering from behavior problems, inattentive, didn't complete class or home learning assignments, and who, as a result of those behaviors, were bringing the school's test scores down. According to the article, in a handwritten note shedding light on the request, the principal wrote, "These are the kids we've got to get outta here if they are low on the FCAT" ("Principal Accused," 2003).

In another not-so-subtle case, Gilman and Reynolds (1991) describe an incident in which a teacher took home completed test answer sheets, ostensibly to clean up erasures and fix stray marks. After the little marks had been "fixed," the class average on the standardized test they had been administered was in the 99th percentile.

Overall, researchers estimate that educators cheat in administering standardized tests in at least 4% to 5% of elementary school classrooms (Jacob & Levitt, 2003). The phenomenon of cheating—on the part of both students and educators–has been described in detail elsewhere (see, e.g., Cizek, 1999, 2001a, 2003a, 2003b). Interested readers are referred to those sources for additional information about specific practices, reasons, and avenues for addressing the problem. For now, we simply conclude that an increasing incidence of inappropriate test behavior is associated with increased anxiety about testing.

Key Idea #12   Test Anxiety Can Affect Teachers and Other Educators By

increasing personal stress levels;

increasing their students' levels of test anxiety ("secondhand stress");

causing or reinforcing negative attitudes toward self or testing;

prompting them to cheat on tests; and

decreasing morale.

Effects on the Classroom

Among the most widely mentioned and notorious effects of test anxiety is the influence of testing on the curriculum and the classroom. For example, anxiety attributable to testing pressures can induce teachers to limit classroom lessons to the content, topics, or skills that are covered by the test (Donegan & Trepanier-Street, 1998; Gilman & Reynolds, 1991; Pedulla et al., 2003; Smith, 1991). This "teaching to the text" phenomenon is familiar to those in the education profession. In some cases, the emphasis on tested content can entirely squeeze out any attention to typically nontested subjects such as social studies, physical education, or art.

Another influence may be that the exclusive focus on tested content reduces a teacher's ability or motivation to innovate, adapt, or stray from the way in which mandated tests assess the approved curriculum. As one researcher phrased it, "multiple-choice testing leads to multiple-choice teaching" (Smith, 1991, p. 10). Such an effect would constrain not only the topics taught in a classroom but also the depth and cognitive complexity (i.e., the higher-order thinking skills) a teacher might otherwise wish to tap.

Although these negative effects of testing and anxiety about testing are real and surely to be avoided, some influences on instruction may actually be positive. For example, the extent to which a teacher provides explicit structure during lessons, (i.e., provides frequent previews and reviews) and reduces the density of instructional input (i.e., avoids "mile-wide, inch-deep" coverage of content) have both been identified as potentially reducing the debilitating effects of test anxiety on student achievement (Helmke, 1988). Furthermore, previewing and reviewing of course material can help promote scaffolding and integration of ideas, can foster conceptual understanding, and can strengthen theoretical frameworks.

Effects on Test Scores

In Chapter 2, we presented a modern definition of test anxiety. What is curious about that definition is that it defines test anxiety exclusively in terms of the affective, physiological, and psychological responses that a person might have to situations in which they are (or perceive themselves to be) evaluated. There is nothing in that definition of test anxiety that says it hurts performance, lowers test scores, or otherwise introduces inaccuracy into the testing process. Certainly, such an omission conflicts with perhaps the primary component of any definition of test anxiety that would result if we asked test takers themselves to develop the definition. According to our commonly held notions, test anxiety is first and foremost a factor that impedes performance and hurts test scores.

Consider, too, a startling statement found in an important study of test anxiety conducted by Hunsley (1985). Hunsley's review of the available evidence on test anxiety yielded the following rather surprising conclusion: "Research therefore does not strongly support the perception of many students and educators that test anxiety has a profound effect on academic performance" (p. 678).

How can this be? Considering all that has just been reviewed about the effects of test anxiety on students and educators, it seems contradictory to assert that common perceptions about test anxiety are simply wrong.

We will attempt to explain these apparent contradictions in the definition of test anxiety, in the research on its effects, and in our classroom observations by digressing for a moment to address two topics. First, we will present a brief and simple statistical explanation of why, though we might observe the debilitating effects of test performance, it can still be true that test anxiety has little effect. Second, we will explore a fundamental concept in testing that we believe should concern all readers, regardless of how many students are affected by test anxiety or how large the effects are.

"On Average, We're Just Fine!"

There is an old though not-very-funny joke amongst statisticians that can help introduce a statistical explanation about why test anxiety does not appear to have a profound effect on student performance. The joke concerns two statisticians who are attending a conference for statisticians and who happen to be assigned to hotel rooms next door to each other. In the room of the first statistician, the temperature is unbearably hot, hovering near 130 degrees Fahrenheit. It is brutally cold in the room of the second statistician, with the thermometer in the room registering –20 degrees. A third statistician happens to come along, and he asks his two colleagues about how comfortable the temperature is in their rooms. "On average, it's great!" they reply.

Of course, this anecdote reflects a truism about the "average" level of something. The average of the two room temperatures—about 75 degrees—obscures the fact that there is a serious discrepancy from that average in both directions. Similarly, the finding that the average effect of test anxiety is not large can, in part, be explained by referring to the well-known U-shaped relationship between anxiety and performance that we presented in Chapter 2. That relationship tells us that test anxiety depresses test performance for students who enter testing situations with a moderate to high level of anxiety to begin with. However, that relationship also tells us that test anxiety actually increases test performance for students who enter testing situations with relatively low levels of test anxiety. Thus, whereas the effect is negative for some, it is positive for others. On average, then, things can appear to be just fine.

A second aspect of this explanation relates to the orientation of people who give tests; that is, of teachers and other educators. We are oriented toward success and toward helping students excel. Barriers to success get our attention. In general, it is probably safe to say that our perceptions are geared more toward observing the negative effects of test anxiety than observing the positive ones. We tend to only take notice of unusual student behaviors and test performances that seem extraordinarily low. We do not tend to notice—and certainly we are not as worried about—student behaviors and test performances that are better than we might have expected.

The Most Fundamental Concern in Testing

As we confessed in the preface of this book, we (the authors) are enamored of testing in a way that distinguishes us from many of our readers. We believe that, for the most part, the work of psychometricians benefits all who are affected by tests. In fact, we believe that the primary concern of testing specialists is one that would be fundamentally shared by almost all educators.

What is this primary concern? In simplistic terms, the singular obsession of testing specialists is an unwavering focus on **error**. Error is a concept that has a specialized meaning for psychometricians. In common usage, an error is a mistake. To a psychometrician, *error* refers to any factor that makes a student's test score higher or lower than the student's "true" level of knowledge or skill. Thus, for example, we might imagine a student who makes numerous lucky guesses on the multiple choice items in a classroom test. The student would be the beneficiary of a considerably higher score than he or she would have obtained without such good luck. Or we might imagine that a student who does not sleep at all on the night before taking the SAT would get a score much lower than expected on that test, due to debilitating fatigue. Both of these situations involve a large error factor. In the first case, error was a factor that resulted in a highly inflated estimate of the student's real achievement; in the second case, an inappropriately low estimate of the student's real ability was the result.

Errors aren't necessarily always of the whopping variety illustrated in these scenarios. Errors also can be very small factors that have very little effect on test scores. For example, small errors occur when a test taker makes just one or two lucky guesses, or when sleep deprivation and momentary inattention cause a test taker to color in bubble B, instead of the (correct) answer they had intended, which was choice C.

Positive or negative. Big or small. Psychometricians have a distaste for all kinds of error. (And, we would like to think that this attitude is shared by all who use or who are affected by tests.) For a psychometrician, the testing utopia is a place where all tests yield accurate results—that is, test scores without error. In the real world, the focus of the work of testing specialists is essentially all about error. We seek to construct tests that are as clear and unambiguous as possible, so that negative error is not introduced through ambiguity or a lack of clarity. We try to develop tests that are free of grammatical or other clues to the correct answer, so that positive errors are not introduced. We seek to craft test items or tasks that are free from bias, so that test takers are not differentially advantaged or disadvantaged by the content or context of the test itself. We try to establish test administration conditions that are free of distractions, that are as immune as possible to cheating, and that are comfortable and safe for all examinees. We insist on objective scoring procedures for multiple-choice (and other **selected-response)** formats, and on training for readers who rate essays (and other **constructed-response** or performance formats), so that fair, accurate, and consistent results are obtained.

The preceding goals—and others—are of paramount importance to testing specialists because there are many potential sources of error that go beyond the two mentioned previously (i.e., guessing and fatigue). And regardless of the size or direction of the effect, errors result in test performances that are not accurate representations of what a student truly knows or can do. This is why we believe that all of us who deal with tests and test takers should be concerned about test anxiety, regardless of how many students are affected or how large the effects are. In the broadest terms, this concern falls under the general heading of **validity**. When a student's test performance is affected by error, the validity of the interpretation of the student's score is weakened.

Validity is a concept that even many nonspecialists in testing have heard about. Certainly, the term itself has a positive connotation in everyday usage. But validity is of special concern to testing specialists. A prominent psychometrician, Robert Ebel, has captured the special place that validity has for those involved in testing, using an imaginative metaphor. He referred to validity as "one of the major deities in the pantheon of the psychometrician" (1961, p. 640). According to the professional standards that apply to educational assessment, "validity is the most fundamental consideration in developing and evaluating tests" (AERA, APA, & NCME, 1999, p. 9). In order to fully grasp the importance of validity as it pertains to the effects of test anxiety, we will go into a bit more depth about this important testing concept.

Strictly speaking, tests and test scores cannot be said to be valid or not valid. Test validity scholar Samuel Messick (1989) is credited as one of the originators of the modern concept of validity as it pertains to the interpretation or **inference** that is made based on test scores. An inference is the interpretation, conclusion, or meaning that a teacher intends to make about a student's knowledge, skill, or ability from the performance. From this perspective, validity refers to the accuracy of the inferences that a teacher wishes to make about a student, usually based on observations of the student's performance—such as on a test, a term paper, or a lab experiment.

Though educators might never state it this technical way, in nearly all cases teachers purposefully design, choose, or administer an assessment precisely to permit such inferences. And most educators never realize that an interpretation of a student's performance or score on a test actually requires an inferential leap; that is, it requires an interpretation of what the student wrote or answered in terms of what the response actually means about the student's level of knowledge, skill, or ability. For example, a composition teacher would be inclined to make the inference from a well-crafted term paper that a student is a thoughtful and well-organized writer. A mathematics teacher would like to make the inferential leap from a student's test paper, in which the student correctly added 20 out of 20 mixed numerals with different denominators, to conclude that the student has solid mastery of that process.

Unfortunately, the inferences a teacher makes are not always the inferences that *can* be made, and our conclusions about students are necessarily tentative. It is a truism: the inferences we can make about a student's ability must be tentative, because we almost never have all of the evidence that would be necessary to proclaim our inference to be a fact.

For example, if the term paper were the product of more parental than student reflection, or more the result of cut-and-pasted organization from an Internet source than of the student's own writing skill, then the inference that the student has strong writing ability would be sketchy. If the perfect performance adding fractions were the result of a lot of lucky guesses, then the inference of "solid mastery" would be incorrect. Similarly, if a student suffered from debilitating test anxiety, then the inference that a fourth-grader has poor reading comprehension, based on a low score on a state-mandated reading test, would also be wrong.

The fact that accurate and meaningful interpretations of test scores rely on the ability to make confident inferences from students' test performances is central to the reason we should be concerned about test anxiety. Any factor that hinders a teacher's, a parent's, or a student's ability to make accurate inferences from a test score threatens validity and jeopardizes the meaningfulness of any conclusions about achievement, ability, progress, or whatever the test is attempting to measure. The bottom line is this: when test anxiety is present, inaccurate inferences can result.

Summary

In the course of this chapter, we presented various estimates of the pervasiveness of test anxiety. We looked at the effects of test anxiety on teachers, test takers, and others. We also explored in some depth the reason that test anxiety should be considered a serious problem; namely, the issue of validity. We learned that current estimates of the incidence of test anxiety are not as precise as we might have hoped. Nonetheless, it is probably safe to say that test anxiety affects about 4 to 6 students in an average classroom. We also learned what those effects are: test anxiety affects not only students but also teachers, other educators, and educational environments, sometimes in very serious ways.

Finally, we explored in depth one of the most familiar effects of test anxiety: poor test performance. From the perspective of testing specialists, the effect of test anxiety lies in inaccurate inferences about students. However, *inaccurate inferences* is not simply a technical expression without real consequence. When test scores lack validity—that is, when they do not mean what we think they mean—there are consequences for students in the form of inaccurate grades, misleading information about one's own knowledge or skill, and potentially erroneous conclusions about the relationships between, for example, effort and results.

When test scores lack validity, there also are consequences for educators, who might adjust lesson plans or assignments for groups or for individual students based on faulty information. Inaccurate inferences can result in making the wrong decisions about students, incorrectly assigning them to gifted programs, mistakenly referring them for special education services, assigning inappropriate grades, and so on.

In a nutshell, the concept of inference has everything to do with the very heart of testing: validity. The issue of validity causes us to be concerned about test anxiety and the ways it can affect test scores, because it can make scores difficult to interpret, possibly inaccurate, and potentially misleading to students, parents, teachers, policymakers, and others who use test scores as part of the decision-making process.

In the course of this chapter, we quoted a few authorities in testing and test anxiety. At this point, we think it is appropriate to refer back to two of those quotes. First, we recall Hunsley's (1985) conclusion that "research therefore does not strongly support the perception of many students and educators that test anxiety has a profound effect on academic performance" (p. 678). Our response to that conclusion is that, although we believe it accurately reflects an overall perspective, it does not necessarily mean that test anxiety does not have profound effects on many individual students. As authors who are ourselves teachers, we believe that educators must be alert to factors that adversely affect the performance of each of our students.

Second, we are reminded of Ebel's (1961) metaphor about the high position of honor afforded to validity by testing specialists. We must now admit, however, that the earlier quotation of Ebel was only part of what he actually said. His major point was not simply to affirm that valid interpretation of test scores is of paramount importance. Here is a fuller version of what Ebel said: "Validity is one of the major deities in the pantheon of the psychometrician. It is universally praised, but the good works done in its name are remarkably few" (p. 640).

What Ebel was trying to say (in 1961) is that whereas everyone might agree that validity is a fundamental characteristic of good testing, the actual hard work of assuring valid test results and accurate interpretations of student performance is more often acknowledged as an ethereal goal than applied as a practical endeavor. A familiar (and somewhat silly) saying about the weather is that "everyone talks about the weather, but no one ever does anything about it." In many cases, the same may be true of validity efforts.

Our general response to Ebel's observation is manifested in this book. Our concern about the validity of test scores leads us to be very concerned about test anxiety. A more specific response is found in Chapter 5. For those readers who are interested in discovering the incidence of test anxiety in their classrooms, buildings, or school districts, Chapter 5 provides a very brief introduction to the measurement of test anxiety, and companion material at the end of the book (Appendix C) provides more detailed information on that topic. Our evaluation of the various test anxiety instruments pays special attention to their validity.

In the best of all worlds, we and (we suspect) the vast majority of educators would dearly like to be able to tell when test anxiety is likely to be a threat to accurate inferences. The information in Chapter 5 may be helpful in identifying specific students who are at particular risk. However, another source of information can help in this regard. In the next chapter, we will look at some of the factors are associated with the presence of test anxiety. These factors can be helpful as signs or rough indicators that test anxiety may be present.

4

The Causes of
Test Anxiety

A s we have already seen, assessing the frequency and potentially serious effects of test anxiety is helpful for understanding the nature and consequences of the phenomenon. Additional insights into the problem can be gleaned from inquiring about the factors related to test anxiety. That is, we can ask: "What characteristics of test takers, their backgrounds, their teachers and classrooms, and so on are related to greater or lesser degrees of test anxiety?"

What Factors Are
Related to Student Test Anxiety?

In this section, we will provide information on the things that are related to test anxiety experienced by students. We will be looking at characteristics of students, their backgrounds, their classrooms, and other factors that seem to go hand in hand with test anxiety. In describing these relationships, we will be relying on existing scientific research that, we fear, might be misconstrued if we are not very careful in the way we present it. We also think it will be helpful if the reader has at least some familiarity with a ubiquitous social science tool—correlation—that is used to discover and estimate the strength of the relationships. The following section may be a light review for some readers or a useful introduction for others.

Correlates, Causes, and Cautions

The major purpose of this chapter is to describe some characteristics of students, classroom environments, and so on that are related to test anxiety. Technically speaking, what we will be describing are relationships between variables. In order to fully understand these relationships, we must digress slightly and provide some requisite background information of a mildly statistical nature.

Don't worry, however! Don't reach for a calculator or run for the door. Our digression is not intended to make statisticians of our readers. Virtually no mathematical proficiency is needed. Absolutely no calculations will be required. As can be verified easily by flipping through the next several pages, we will be treating our only mildly statistical topic nearly without numbers. Instead, simply acquiring a basic conceptual grasp of the way social scientists study relationships between things such as, for example, test anxiety and grades is all that is needed to have a fairly sophisticated understanding of test anxiety.

The Concept of Correlation

When social scientists talk about relationships between variables, they often use the technical term *correlates*. In addressing the topic of factors related to test anxiety, it is critical to first be clear about an important distinction—the difference between correlates and causes.[1]

Many readers may be familiar with the related term **correlation** from a course in statistics, testing, or research methods. A correlate is a variable that is related to another variable. For example, for high school–aged students, the hours students spend working in a job during the school year is a correlate of GPA. That is, there is a relationship between the two variables, hours working and GPA, and we would say that the variables are correlated. Nearly all of the information we have about characteristics of students and test anxiety is called correlational evidence. A good understanding of how to interpret correlational evidence is essential to accurately interpreting the research on characteristics related to test anxiety.

Correlation is a statistical technique used to determine the strength of any relationship that might exist between two variables. If we calculated a correlation between two variables, we would come up with a number that would range from −1.0 to +1.0. Negative correlations indicate that high values on one of the variables tend to be associated with low values on the other variable.

For example, let us continue the example we began earlier and suppose that we collected data for a group of high school seniors on two variables: hours per week spent working during the school year and GPA. These variables are correlated in a negative way. If we were to actually calculate a correlation (don't worry, we won't), it is likely that there would be a strong negative relationship between these variables. The calculation would yield a number close to −1.0. We would interpret that negative correlation to mean that students with a higher number of hours worked per week would tend to have lower GPAs. Conversely, students with a lower number of hours worked per week would tend to have higher GPAs. Such a relationship, if perfect, could be illustrated by a straight, sloping line, similar to the one illustrated in Figure 4–1(a).

However, suppose we collected data on the same students on two different variables: high school GPA and total score on the SAT. These variables are correlated, too, but in a positive way. If we calculated a correlation based on this data, the calculation would yield a number close to +1.0. We would interpret this strong positive correlation to mean that students with higher GPAs have, on average, higher SAT scores. And students with lower GPAs would tend to have lower SAT scores. Again, if this positive relationship were perfect, the values would fall along a straight line, this time sloping in the opposite direction from that seen in the case of a negative relationship. A perfect positive relationship is shown in Figure 4–1(b).

In just a bit, we will begin describing some of the correlates of test anxiety; that is, we will be reviewing what we know about characteristics that are related to test anxiety and the ways in which those characteristics are related (i.e., positively or negatively). However, now that we have explained what we mean by the concept of correlation, we must offer some cautions about interpreting correlations.

Although correlations can range from −1.0 to +1.0, most of the time they are closer to the middle of that range, which is 0.0. Correlations close to the extremes of −1.0 and +1.0 are actually very rare, and the relationships we see are almost never perfect. For example, in the context of our example, a perfect positive correlation between GPA and SAT would occur only when the student with the highest GPA had the highest SAT score, the student with the second-highest GPA had the second-highest SAT score, and so on for every student in our sample, so that the pairs of GPA and SAT scores fell neatly along the straight line shown on the graph in Figure 4–1(b).

Such a result is extremely rare, however, because there are almost always exceptions to even the strongest relationships. All it would

Figure 4–1   Hypothetical Illustrations of Correlations

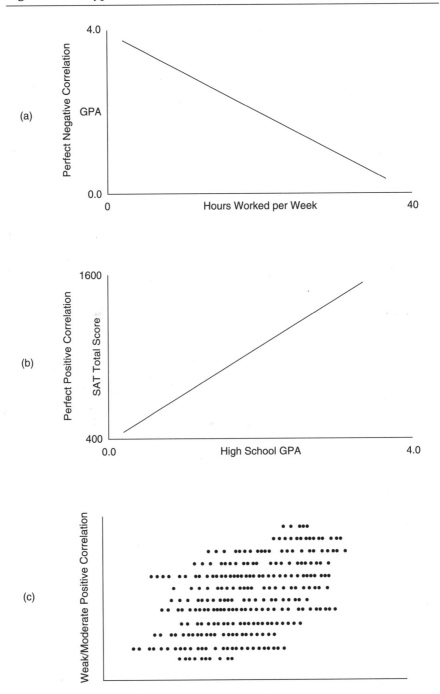

take for the correlation in our sample of high school students to be less than +1.0 would be for one student with a high GPA to do poorly on his or her SAT. The more the pairs of data are dispersed like this, the less the graph of the data will look like a straight line (it would

---

O━▥ **Key Idea #13   Correlations . . .**

- are a statistical technique for expressing how strongly two things (variables) are related to each other;

- are numbers ranging between negative 1.0 and positive 1.0;

- can be positive—that is, between 0.0 and 1.0—when two variables are associated in the same way as, for example, height and shoe size are related (taller people tend to have bigger feet, and shorter people tend to have smaller feet);

- can be negative—that is, between –1.0 and 0.0—when two variables are inversely associated as, for example, hours of television watching and grades are related (students who watch greater amounts of television tend to have lower grades, and those who watch lower amounts of television tend to have higher grades);

- can be zero (0.0) when there is no relationship; and

- reveal stronger relationships the closer the calculated correlations are to the extremes of –1.0 and +1.0.

---

look more like a scattering of points in an oval shape) and the closer to zero the correlation would be. An example of a more typical relationship (i.e., a weak to moderate positive correlation, greater than 0.0 but less than +1.0) is illustrated in Figure 4–1(c).

Four Caveats About Correlations

Having acquired a basic understanding of correlation, we must always be concerned that correlational information is interpreted accurately. There are four critical cautions to remember.

Our first caution for interpreting correlational evidence is this: *correlations are about groups, not about individuals*. There are always exceptions to the general tendency represented by the correlation. Knowing, for example, that there is a very strong positive correlation between GPA and SAT score (say +.95) doesn't tell us anything about any particular student. That is, just because we know that a particular student has a high GPA does not necessarily guarantee that the student also has (or will have) a high SAT score. This caution is important for interpreting the correlational evidence about test anxiety. There may be a negative relationship between grades and test anxiety (in fact, there is); however, that does not mean that a student who has low grades suffers from greater test anxiety.

The second caution regarding correlations is this: *the size of the correlation matters.* As we just mentioned, correlations near the extremes (i.e., near −1.0 or near +1.0) indicate very strong relationships and very strong tendencies, and such correlations are very rare. Most of the time in the social sciences, we observe correlations much closer to zero. A correlation of 0.0 indicates that there is no relationship between the two variables.[2] Weak positive or weak negative correlations (say, near .25 or −.25) are much more common than stronger ones. Weak correlations mean that the relationships between the variables are very slight or hard to detect, or that there are likely a large number of other variables that contribute as much or more to the relationship.

For example, there is actually a very weak positive correlation between height and IQ (near +.05). What do we do with such information? Almost certainly there are other factors that contribute to individual differences in height and intelligence. And it is likely that some other unidentified variable accounts for the relationship (e.g., prenatal nutrition). The press might find such a correlation to be mildly interesting and may even sensationalize the relationship in a few-second blurb on a news program or magazine. And social scientists would probably continue to investigate the relationship and speculate about why even such slight correlation exists. But for the most part, people—especially teachers—could and probably should ignore the finding because the tendency is so weak.

This second caution is also important for understanding the characteristics of students who suffer from test anxiety. Like most other correlational evidence in the social sciences, the calculated correlations between some personal characteristic and test anxiety are usually quite modest. Again, this means that even when tendencies are identified they usually are weak ones. Some are, arguably, strong enough to warrant our attention; others are weak enough that we may safely ignore them.

A third caution related to interpreting correlational evidence is this: *even the strongest correlation does not indicate that one of the variables causes the other.* For example, let us suppose that we have a very strong negative correlation (say, −.95) between two variables, hours per week worked during the school year and high school grades. Despite the fact that this correlation is indeed very strong, we still can't conclude anything about whether there is a cause-and-effect relationship operating. That is, we don't necessarily know if working a lot of hours during school causes low grades (e.g., because students have little time left to study or to do homework) or if students with low grades decide to work more (because school doesn't seem to be going too well for them). One variable *might* cause the other, but we don't know. In fact, it may even be the case that neither variable causes the other; there may be a third variable that affects both hours worked and grades.

For example, family income level is frequently mentioned as being related to success in school. Though grades are surely the result of the contributions of many factors, a child from a poor family might have low grades, in part, because his or her family lacks the resources to acquire extra tutoring or outside educational opportunities. Nonetheless, the student may not get higher grades even if the family's income level were suddenly increased, because the family would still have the freedom to make choices about how to spend the additional income; the student's grades may go up, go down, or change not at all as a result of those choices. Thus, income level alone cannot be called a "cause" of higher or lower grades.

Or suppose that the same student needed to work to help offset family living expenses, or simply to afford the kinds of discretionary purchases that students from wealthier families can purchase with money given to them by their parents. In this situation, despite a strong correlation between hours worked per week and grades, neither variable would be causing the other; instead, a third variable—family income level—might account for the relationship between the two.

The application of this principle to test anxiety should be clear. Does the fact that a student tends to have poor grades cause him or her to be more anxious about test situations, or does being anxious in test situations cause poorer performance and, hence, lower grades? In summary, the caution here is that we must be very careful before concluding that one variable causes another (i.e., that there is a causal relationship between the two variables).

A fourth and final caution is this: *even if we believe that a causal relationship exists, it is another matter to discover the direction of the cause and effect.* To illustrate this principle, one of the authors (GJC) will recall his own training to become an elementary school teacher.

That training occurred during the late 1970s—a time when the relationship between two variables, self-concept and achievement, was the subject of concerted research. I recall being taught, correctly, that there was a correlation between students' self-concept and academic achievement. I don't think anyone ever taught me that the relationship was causal, though it seemed as if everyone acted as if that were the case. We were explicitly taught to try to boost students' self-concept so that it might result in greater academic achievement for them. I even recall lessons that we were told would help students get that needed boost in self-concept, such as class activities in which students would "say something nice" about another student. One particularly memorable (or forgettable) lesson involved having students wear little placards around their necks that read "IALAC." That acronym, we were supposed to tell our young students, meant "I am lovable and capable"—just the self-concept–boosting message that would surely send math scores shooting upward, or so we were led to believe.

Our training was correct in one respect: there is a relationship between self-concept and academic achievement. The correlation is positive and fairly strong, meaning that students with higher academic achievement tend to have higher self-concepts, and vice versa. Where we were mistaken was in assessing the direction of the effect. In fact, as subsequent research has clarified, trying to "teach" self-concept is largely ineffective. Students know the truth and we can't kid them. A student who doesn't understand how to divide fractions is not going to notice a surge in her math problem-solving skills just because we tell her that she is lovable and capable. It is a student's personal experience of success in challenging academic work—actually experiencing that he or she can invert, multiply, and get the correct answer—that leads to an increase in her self-concept.

Obviously, sometimes we *can* be very sure about the presence or direction of a causal relationship; there are instances in which the direction of a relationship can only be in one direction. Suppose we were looking at the relationship between a background characteristic of students—for example, sex—and degree of test anxiety. There may be some doubt about whether test anxiety is a sex-linked characteristic (that is, we may not know whether being a boy or a girl *causes* a person to have more test anxiety). However, we would be certain about the direction of the relationship; that is, it is not possible that having more test anxiety causes a person to be a boy or a girl! The bottom line for this fourth caution is that we should always be vigilant about avoiding the impulse to jump to conclusions about direction of effect or causation.

At last! Our brief foray into statistics is complete. (It wasn't that bad, was it?) We have examined perhaps the most common statistical tool that researchers use to describe relationships—correlations. And we have outlined four important cautions to bear in mind when

Key Idea #14   Four Cautions About Correlations

1. Correlations are about groups, not individuals. Unless a correlation is perfect (i.e., −1.0 or +1.0), many people will not fit the pattern exactly or may even be an opposite of the general tendency described by a correlation.

2. The size of the correlation matters. Correlations closer to the extremes of −1.0 and +1.0 reveal stronger relationships.

3. Correlations do not indicate causes. Even the strongest correlational relationships do not tell us whether one variable causes the other. In many cases, the relationship between two things may be the result of an unknown third factor that causes both of them.

4. Correlations do not indicate the direction of a relationship. For example, grades may be strongly related to the number of hours a student spends studying, but we can't be sure whether getting good grades prompts some students to study hard or studying hard promotes better grades.

interpreting correlations. We now turn to an overview of the correlates of test anxiety.

Relationships With Test Anxiety

Test anxiety is, as some would say, well connected. In this section, we will try to define that relationship.

Generally speaking, test anxiety does not usually operate alone; in most cases, it is closely related to other factors or variables that are also at work. It's hard to say who invited whom—did test anxiety initiate the party or was it invited? Researchers have not discovered definitive answers to questions about how test anxiety is related to other variables, but they have identified several key influences, and many are the usual suspects—like age, sex, ethnicity, and socioeconomic status (SES). However, one might not have guessed the identity of a few of the other guests, such as family environment, self-esteem, and subject matter. Test anxiety's connection with other variables is not just domestic, and there appear to be some interesting cross-cultural relationships. It also seems that test anxiety has a significant relationship with teacher-manifested anxiety.

Before we start dissecting this network of relationships, let us consider the findings displayed in Table 4–1, using the information about correlations presented previously in this chapter as background and adding one new bit of requisite information. The new piece of information has to do with a second way (in addition to correlations) that statisticians describe the strength of a relationship, called an **effect size**. An effect size is sometimes used to describe how much of a difference a certain variable makes in the relationship. For example, two variables such as hours spent doing homework and high school GPA might be very strongly correlated (+.80), but the affect on GPA of doing each additional hour of homework might be very small (a small effect size). Or doing an additional hour of homework each night might be associated with a substantial increase in GPA (a large effect size).

Effect sizes are reported on a standard scale, ranging from essentially –2.0 (extremely large negative effect of the variable) to +2.0 (extremely large positive effect of the variable), where a tenth of a unit is usually considered to be a meaningfully large effect. For example, if we imagine cutting up the –2.0 to +2.0 scale into tenths, that would result in 40 steps or increments along the way. Loosely speaking, an effect size of .10 would represent a difference of about 1/40th of the total possible influence. If a variable has no effect, its effect size would be in the middle of that scale: zero.

Table 4–1, based on a summary of over 500 studies of test anxiety involving over 900 correlations and compiled by Hembree (1988), presents an overview of the relationships (i.e., the correlates) and the influence (i.e., the effect sizes) of test anxiety. The table gives us an idea of the factors that are most strongly related to test anxiety, an idea about the factors that tend not to be related to test anxiety at all, and an idea about how great the influence of any relationship is.

With Whom Does Test Anxiety Like to Hang Out?

Test anxiety shows favoritism. More elementary and middle school teachers than high school teachers report that their students are anxious and under pressure. In general, test anxiety prefers the company of students in the early grades, and girls mostly.

Age/Grade Level

Figure 4–2 shows average levels of test anxiety, gleaned from studies that measured test anxiety in students across Grades 1 though 12, and broken down by sex. Overall, for both boys and

Table 4–1   Correlates of Test Anxiety

Correlate	Mean Correlation (r) or Effect Size (ES)	Interpretation
Sex		
Grades 1–2	ES = 0.14	The effect of test anxiety tends to be greatest for females across all elementary and secondary grades, extending into postsecondary settings. However, the effect of test anxiety on female students tends to be greatest in the middle school and early high school years and weakest in early elementary school and college.
Grades 3–4	ES = 0.28	
Grades 5–10	ES = 0.43	
Grades 11+	ES = 0.27	
Ethnicity (African American/White)		
Grades 2–4	ES = 0.52	There is a very large test anxiety difference between Black and White students in the elementary grades, with Black students showing greater test anxiety; the effect size shrinks to essentially zero (meaning no difference in test anxiety) by high school.
Grades 5–8	ES = 0.21	
Grades 9–12	ES = 0.02	
(Hispanic/White)		
Grades 4–12	ES = 0.36	Across all studies of the differences in test anxiety between Hispanic and White students, a fairly consistent and greater level of test anxiety is shown by Hispanic students.
Socioeconomic Status (SES)	r = −0.13	Higher SES level is weakly associated with lower level of test anxiety.

(Continued)

Table 4–1 (Continued)

Correlate	Mean Correlation (r) or Effect Size (ES)	Interpretation
Ability		
High vs. Average	ES = –0.49	Test anxiety is much greater for average ability students compared to high ability students, and much greater for low ability students than for average ability students.
Low vs. Average	ES = 0.52	
IQ	r = –0.10/–0.23	In studies at the early elementary/later elementary through college, higher test anxiety levels are weakly associated with higher IQ.
GPA	r = –0.12 (high school) r = –0.29 (college) ES = –0.46 (college)	In both high school and college, higher levels of test anxiety tend to be associated with lower GPAs. In studies of college students, there is a fairly large negative impact on GPA associated with test anxiety.
Subject Area Achievement		
Reading/English	r = –0.24 (Grades 3+)	Across subject areas, there is a fairly consistent, though weak to modest, tendency for higher achievement in the subject to be associated with lower levels of test anxiety, and vice versa.
Mathematics	r = –0.22 (Grades 4+)	
Natural Sciences	r = –0.21 (college)	
Social Sciences	r = –0.25 (Grades 5+)	
Foreign Languages	r = –0.12 (college)	
General Anxiety Level	r = 0.56	Across grades 1–12, students who are more anxious in general tend to have greater levels of test anxiety.

Correlate	Mean Correlation (r) or Effect Size (ES)	Interpretation
Study Skills	r = −0.27	Studies conducted at the high school level indicate that better study skills are associated with reduced test anxiety
Self-Esteem	r = −0.42	Higher self-esteem is fairly strongly associated with lower test anxiety
Divergent Thinking	r = −0.07	Very weak to no relationship between divergent thinking style and test anxiety
Need for Achievement		
Grades 4–8	r = −0.16	In the elementary grades, a higher need for achievement is associated with lower test anxiety. That pattern reverses in high school. There is essentially no relationship between these variables in college.
Grades 10–12	r = 0.26	
College	r = 0.03	
Perceived Test Difficulty	ES = 0.35	Perception that a test is hard has fairly large effect on level of test anxiety
Test Item Format	ES = −0.58	Matching format has large negative (reducing) effect on less test anxiety compared to multiple-choice format
Familiarity of Environment (e.g., grade level transition)	ES = −0.01	Assignment to new school building versus assignment to familiar school building has essentially no effect on test anxiety
Student At-Risk Status	ES = 0.51	At risk students have substantially higher levels of test anxiety
Teacher Anxiety	r = 0.64	Greater teacher anxiety strongly related to greater student test anxiety

SOURCE: Adapted from Hembree (1988).

Figure 4–2   Average Test-Anxiety Levels for Grades 1 Through 12

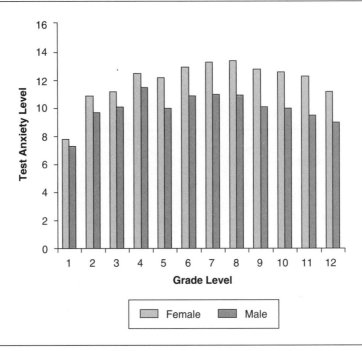

girls, test anxiety appears to be at its lowest level when students first begin schooling; the level increases through the early grades, stabilizes during the middle school years, and begins to taper off when students enter high school. These results generally confirm what teachers report: upper elementary school teachers report more anxiety and stress in their students than do lower elementary teachers. The results of one survey of teachers revealed that 82% of elementary school teachers, 77% of middle school teachers, and 69% of high school teachers agreed with the statement "Many students are extremely anxious about taking the state-mandated test" (Pedulla et al., 2003). Results from a similar study, shown in Table 4–2, indicate that a majority of both lower and upper elementary school teachers reported observing student stress during testing at least occasionally, and a large percentage reported observing student stress frequently.

A number of hypotheses have been suggested to try to explain the inverted U-shaped relationship between age/grade level and test anxiety. For example, one reason that levels of test anxiety may be lower in college students might be that, in general, highly test-anxious

Table 4–2   Percentage of Teachers Reporting Incidences of Student Stress During Standardized Testing

	Reported Incidence		
Grade Range	*Never*	*Occasionally*	*Frequently/Consistently*
Lower Elementary	31.9%	55.3%	12.8%
Upper Elementary	7.0%	75.4%	17.5%

SOURCE: Adapted from Donegan and Trepanier-Street (1998)

students elect not to attend college (which would subject them to more testing). Thus, the apparent decline in test anxiety at the post-secondary level may be less a developmental trend than it is the result of attrition. Another explanation may simply be related to the well-known phenomenon that measurements of nearly all psychological variables tend to increase in accuracy and reliability with the age of respondents. Zeidner (1998) has summarized other possible explanations for the increase in test anxiety through the grade levels:

- Increasing demands and pressures for academic accomplishments from parents and teachers over the school years.
- Greater complexity of learning materials and tasks across the grade levels, which could have the effect of reducing students' expectations of success, thereby increasing test anxiety.
- A cumulative effect of failures, poor performance on tests, and the detrimental effects of aversive, anxiety-evoking evaluations.
- A decrease in students' levels of defensiveness as they age, resulting in a corresponding increase in their willingness to report their levels of test anxiety. (p. 270)

Subject Area

Some varieties of test anxiety appear to be more commonly encountered than others, and the mathematics test anxiety reaction of Peppermint Patty (Figure 4–3) is one that most teachers have probably observed in their students. Researchers have investigated the hypothesis that test anxiety is more likely to be experienced in some subject areas than in others. Within the circle of those who study test anxiety for a living (there is, for example, a professional association

Figure 4–3

SOURCE: Peanuts, by Charles M. Schulz, © UFS, Inc. Reprinted by permission.

called the Society for Test Anxiety Research[3]), subfields of study in test anxiety have sprung up, including math test anxiety, statistics test anxiety, and others (although we have not encountered any specialists in either poetry test anxiety or home economics test anxiety).

In theory at least, test anxiety should be aroused in any context in which the worry and emotionality associated with negative evaluation (or fear of negative evaluation) are aroused. Thus, also theoretically, true test anxiety should not be subject-specific unless a particular subject area is more likely to provoke such states. Indeed, looking again at Table 4–1, we see that the relationships between test anxiety levels and achievement in subject areas such as reading, mathematics, natural science, and social science are remarkably homogenous—all are negative and in the weak to moderate range—just as might be predicted based on the theory. In short, higher achievement scores tend to be obtained by students with lower levels of test anxiety, and lower achievement tends to be associated with higher levels of test anxiety, regardless of subject area. Or, put another way, the level of test anxiety does not appear to depend on what kind of test a student is "subject-ed" to (sorry, but we couldn't resist such a pun, no matter how much of a groaner it is).

Slightly more recent data are available on the relationship between achievement and test anxiety at the college level. In one study, researchers found that students were more anxious when tests involved subjects like mathematics or physical science and experienced less test anxiety in subjects such as English or social science (Everson, Tobias, Hartman, & Gourgey, 1993), though these data also differ in that the researchers relied on students' self-reported levels of test anxiety, instead of measuring it directly. Also, it may not matter whether the subject area is truly or inherently more difficult, intimidating, challenging, or complex; higher test anxiety appears to be associated with what students *think* about the subject. As Everson et al. report: "Students' perceptions of a subject's difficulty were related positively to their reported levels of test anxiety" (p. 4).

Teacher Anxiety

In a previous section, we described the effects of testing on teachers. We noted that teachers, though they do not take tests directly, nonetheless experience stress and anxiety as participants in high-stakes testing situations, and they experience the pressures of educational accountability systems. Interestingly, of all the relationships shown in Table 4–1, perhaps none is more striking than the correlation between teacher anxiety and student test anxiety. This strong correlation ($r = 0.64$) is the strongest relationship yet found between student test anxiety and any other variable. Again, we are reminded that even very strong correlations do not imply that one variable causes higher or lower test anxiety, but this relationship is large and worthy of special mention. In Chapter 6, we will examine in greater detail what teachers might do based on this relationship.

Sex

A look back at Table 4–1 (or at Figure 4–2) confirms that, among other relationships, test anxiety is greater in females than in males, regardless of grade level (although some researchers have wondered whether it is the differences that are pronounced or whether females are simply more apt to report anxious feelings). The association between sex and test anxiety tends to be greatest in the middle school and early high school grades, and weakest in the early elementary grades.

This gender difference in test anxiety is a topic of continuing research, and some possible explanations for the difference have been suggested. For example, recall that in Chapter 2, during our formal definition of test anxiety, we described its worry and emotionality components. Females appear to experience higher emotionality than worry. One hypothesis is that women react to evaluative settings as more threatening, whereas men may be more likely to treat a test situation as a personal challenge. Thus, in identical situations, men may tend to exhibit the facilitating responses of test anxiety (the "good" anxiety), whereas women would react with the more of the debilitating effect of test anxiety. Another hypothesis is that women are simply more likely to report test anxiety than men, who tend to be more defensive and to exhibit the culturally taught response of suppressing acknowledgment of anxiety.

Key Idea #15   Test Anxiety Is Most Commonly Seen in Students Who . . .

- are female;
- are African American or Hispanic;
- have average ability;
- have low GPAs;
- are generally anxious;
- have poor study skills;
- have low self-esteem;
- perceive that a test will be hard;
- have just moved into a new school; or
- have teachers who are anxious about testing.

Other Relationships

Several other interesting relationships can be seen in Table 4–1. For example, we note that test anxiety appears to be related in the following ways:

- Higher test-anxiety levels are associated with lower IQ scores and with lower scores on other **ability tests**.
- Higher test anxiety is associated with lower GPAs and poorer study skills.
- Higher test anxiety is associated with lower self-esteem and higher levels of general anxiety, and people with a "feeling" style on the Myers-Briggs Type Indicator had higher levels of test anxiety than those classified as having a "thinking" style (Shermis & Lombard, 1998).
- Higher levels of test anxiety are associated with perceptions of greater test difficulty, multiple-choice test formats, and highly prescriptive testing practices (e.g., instructions that indicate a test will require specific correct answers and that rely heavily on knowledge of information and rules) (Everson, Tobias, Hartman, & Gourgey, 1991).

Where in the World Is Test Anxiety?

Test anxiety also has a passport, so to speak. The finding that females exhibit higher levels of test anxiety than males has been observed

Figure 4–4   Cross-Cultural Comparison of Gender Differences in
Test Anxiety

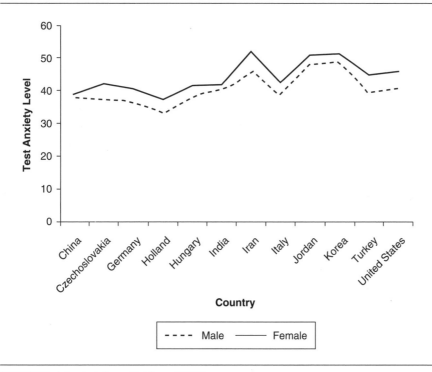

SOURCE: Adapted from Zeidner (1998).

across the globe. A cross-cultural comparison of gender group differences in test anxiety is presented in Figure 4–4. The figure is based on
studies conducted in 12 countries, involving elementary, middle, and
high school students whose level of test anxiety was measured using
the *Test Anxiety Inventory* (Spielberger, 1977). As the figure shows, in
every country, the test anxiety levels of females exceeded those of
their male counterparts in elementary and secondary school settings.
And although it is not shown in this figure, the same pattern of differences was observed in 12 countries in which test anxiety was studied at the college level. Given the diversity of the cultures in which
these gender-difference studies were conducted, it is clear (though
not reassuring) that higher levels of test anxiety in women are neither
a uniquely Western phenomenon nor a by-product of the American
educational system.

There are, of course, more cross-cultural differences to explore, as
well as examining the relationship between test anxiety and ethnicity
and SES. It is somewhat complicated to separate out the individual
effect of a variable (e.g., sex) when culture, ethnicity, SES, and other

variables are themselves interrelated and share an association with test anxiety. Complicated, intertwined effects such as these are regularly studied by social scientists are referred to as *interactions* (if the effect of one variable depends on the presence or magnitude of another factor) or as *confounded* (if the effect of one variable cannot be disentangled from another). The different, complex ways in which variables such as these relate to one another helps explain why research findings sometimes lead social scientists to different conclusions and explanations for the same phenomenon. In the following paragraphs, however, we do our best to summarize the current state of what is known about the relationship of test anxiety to other commonly studied variables of interest.

SES

One study comparing seventh- and eighth-grade students in North America and Chile found that low-SES students in both cultures appear to suffer from higher levels of test anxiety than do middle-SES and upper-SES students (Guida & Ludlow, 1989). As might be expected, based on the single relationship between sex and test anxiety, higher levels of test anxiety were found in low-SES females than in low-SES males. And (as might be expected because of the complicated ways in which variables interact) upper- and middle-class Chilean students were found to suffer from higher levels of test anxiety than did similar U.S. students.

Looking again in Table 4–1, we note that overall there is a very small, negative correlation between test anxiety level and SES ($r = -0.13$). That is, there is a slight tendency for a lower SES to be associated with a higher test-anxiety level. The effect is small enough that it may not lead to any practical differences in how teachers can help students deal with test anxiety (see Chapter 6). However, researchers have offered some hypotheses for why even these small relationships exist. For example, Zeidner has suggested that "due to the conflict between school and lower-class minority home cultures, lower-class students may experience more failure, frustration, and punitive experiences in schools than middle-class children, thus elevating their levels of test anxiety" (1998, p. 271).

Ethnicity

Ethnicity is among the most studied variables in research conducted in the United States. Test-anxiety levels have been examined for three large ethnic groups: Whites, African Americans, and Hispanics. Of course, many more ethnic groups can be found in U.S. classrooms, but the major reason that studies of other groups have not been conducted has more to do with the difficulties of gathering data and size of an ethnic group than with any other factor.

Nonetheless, solid information is available for at least a few groups. As is evident from the effect sizes presented in Table 4–1, African American students display higher test anxiety levels than do White students in early grades, but that difference narrows during middle school and is virtually nonexistent by high school, where African American and White students appear to experience about the same average levels of test anxiety (Crocker, Schmitt, & Tang, 1988; Hembree, 1988). However, the effect size at the early elementary level (ES = 0.52) is substantial and reveals a markedly negative effect of test anxiety for African American students compared to Whites.

A smaller, though still sizeable difference in test anxiety between White and Hispanic students (ES = 0.36) can also be seen in Table 4–1. Interestingly, however, test anxiety levels were found to be higher for students in Mexico than for students in the United States (Holtzman, Diaz-Guerrero, & Swartz, 1975, cited in Guida & Ludlow, 1989). Researchers theorize two causes for this. First, it may be that stress and anxiety are passively endured in Mexican culture, which results in a low threshold for active stress and anxiety. A second possibility may be that a greater emphasis is placed on obedience to adult authorities in Mexican cultures and therefore evaluations and tests pose a greater threat to Mexican students, resulting in higher test anxiety. To some extent, these hypotheses may carry over to Hispanic students in U.S. schools.

Finally, as we mentioned previously, researchers often can obtain different results or come to different conclusions because of what we called *interaction effects*. This is the case with ethnicity and grade level. Recall that earlier we saw that levels of test anxiety are generally greater in elementary and middle school than in high schools. And we just learned that test anxiety levels are generally greater for African American students than for White students. An example of the interaction of these variables is found in the conclusions offered by Turner et al. (1993), who observe that

> the prevalence of test anxiety in urban African American children attending an elementary school in a lower socioeconomic area is not significantly different from the prevalence of

children attending a suburban and mostly white school district in a middle- to upper-middle class area, or a racially mixed and socioeconomically mixed school district. . . . The pervasive effects of test anxiety appear to be similar without regard to race. (p. 148)

Clearly, these variables—grade level and ethnicity—can be intertwined, and we cannot (without more definitive research to isolate the effects) confidently ascribe some percentage of test-anxiety level to the first variable and another percentage to the second.

Is Test Anxiety in the Genes?

We suspect that far too many teachers have heard parents explain to their child: "Don't worry; I was no good at math either, so you probably got that from me." Of course, educators know that, contrary to the beliefs of some, there is no such thing as a gene for mathematical aptitude. Math achievement depends as much or more on effort, practice, persistence, and so on than it does on whatever DNA Billy inherited from Mom and Dad.

Similarly, there is no such thing as a test-anxiety gene or being a naturally poor test taker. Nonetheless, saying that test anxiety is not a genetically transmitted characteristic is not the same as saying it has nothing to do with one's parents. In fact, it does. Test anxiety is strongly related to parents—not in the biologically determined sense, but in the sense of family relationships and family environment. For example, one recent study of sixth-, tenth-, and twelfth-graders (Chapell & Overton, 1998) investigated the effects of parenting styles on two variables: test-anxiety level and reasoning. Using a parenting-style instrument, the authors classified parents as either authoritative or nonauthoritative based on their total scores. Authoritative parents were described as those who were "responsive, supportive, democratic yet demanding"; nonauthoritative parents included those whose parenting styles were described as authoritarian, indulgent, or neglectful. The researchers found that "authoritative parenting was related to more advanced reasoning performance and lower test anxiety that was nonauthoritative parenting" (p. 141).

As early as 1960, leading researchers on test anxiety hypothesized that test anxiety results from interactions early in life between a child and his or her parents (Sarason, Davidson, Lighthall, Waite, & Ruebush, 1960). Following up on those early hypotheses, several current theories of test anxiety maintain that test anxiety originates when a parent's overly high academic expectations or demands are expressed during their child's early school years (Hill & Wigfield, 1984; McDonald, 2001). Thus a cycle begins: the child cannot always meet the parent's overly high expectations; parents react negatively to the child's failure to meet those expectations; the child in turn becomes more fearful of tests and adults' reactions to his or her academic performance. For a child, then, parental expectations, valuing of education, and support for achievement may be both one of the greatest incentives for success and one of the greatest potential predictors of test anxiety, if those expectations are unrealistic. Parents who develop and maintain positive relationships with their children can potentially foster successful academic performance and a minimal level of test anxiety (Sapp, 1999).

Other family-related factors also influence test anxiety. For example, results of a study of adolescent children indicated that children of divorced parents had significantly higher test-anxiety levels that did children of intact families (Guttman, 1987). Further, family environment (as measured by family communication, encouragement of personal growth, and family system maintenance) was found to be inversely related to children's test anxiety and trait anxiety (Peleg-Popko & Klingman, 2002). In other words, children's test anxiety and fears were negatively correlated with family relationships. In general, the poorer the family relationships, the greater the level of test anxiety. Overall, it would appear that the greater the levels of anxiety in children's lives—regardless of whether the source of that anxiety is within the school walls or outside them—the greater the potential for students to be susceptible to test anxiety.

Summary

In this chapter we looked at a number of variables that seem to be associated with test anxiety. We also identified some variables that have been shown to be unrelated to test anxiety. Finally, we gained some idea about the relative effect of certain factors on levels of test anxiety.

With a clear understanding of what test anxiety is, how it affects students, and how some characteristics are (or are not) related to test anxiety, we must consider only one more question before getting to the important issue of addressing test anxiety: how can we know how great or how slight a student's level of test anxiety is? In the next chapter, we will provide a brief introduction to measuring test anxiety, as a way of shedding light on that question. Then, in Chapter 6, we will use all of what we have learned to try to provide concrete, practical ways that educators, parents, and students can help reduce test anxiety.

Notes

1. The following discussion on correlates and causes is taken from Cizek (2003a).

2. For our purposes, this statement is accurate enough. However, a more technically precise rendering would note that a correlation of 0.0 means that there is no *linear* relationship between the variables.

3. In 1991, the group officially changed its name to the Stress and Anxiety Research Society but retained the acronym STAR, associated with the old name. In retrospect, retaining the old acronym was probably a better choice than changing to the acronym that would be formed from the new name (SARS). For the interested reader, additional information on STAR is provided in Appendix B.

5

Measuring
Test Anxiety

For anyone interested in addressing test anxiety in general, the first step is to gain an understanding of the phenomenon, and we have tried to promote a deeper understanding of test anxiety in the preceding chapters. The next step would be to try to provide some relief to the individual students affected by test anxiety, and it would probably make the most sense to focus on those test takers for whom test anxiety problems are the most debilitating.

But how do we know which students are most affected by test anxiety? As we learned in Chapter 4, there are certainly correlational relationships that demand our attention—such as females having generally higher levels of test anxiety than males—but these relationships are subject to the cautions of correlations. Among those cautions is the truism that correlations tell us something about groups, on average, but nothing about any specific student in particular.

Fortunately, researchers and testing specialists have developed a number of ways to measure test anxiety. As it turns out—ironically, perhaps—what have been developed are test-anxiety tests. Our purpose in this chapter is to introduce the reader to the basics of test-anxiety measurement. For the reader who is interested in greater depth on this topic, we have included a related appendix (Appendix C), which provides the actual directions and real sample questions from several test-anxiety instruments. In the appendix, we also provide information on the technical quality of the available instruments, to aid the reader in choosing and using an instrument appropriately.

The Roots of Measuring Test Anxiety

The origin of test-anxiety instruments can be traced to the early 1950s. Perhaps the first instrument was the *Test Anxiety Questionnaire* (TAQ) (Mandler & Sarason, 1952), based on an early theory of test anxiety. The TAQ consisted of 37 items and was designed to gauge the extent to which test takers engaged in actions that were either helpful toward completing the task at hand (task-relevant behaviors) or that hindered successful task completion (task-irrelevant behaviors). A descendant of the TAQ, the *Test Anxiety Scale* (TAS) (Sarason, 1958), was developed to improve upon the measurement of test anxiety afforded by the TAQ. The 1958 version of the TAS comprised 21 items; a later version comprises 37 items (Sarason, 1978). Each of the items is a single statement; the student selects *true* if the statement describes him or her, *false* if it does not.

As test-anxiety instruments go, the TAS is perhaps the granddaddy of them all, although it has essentially fallen out of use. Compared to the test-anxiety instruments of today, the TAS is comparatively rudimentary and is based on an outmoded theory of test anxiety. No technical manual or **norms** are available for the TAS, and only the most basic information on reliability and validity is contained in various publications (see, e.g., Sarason, 1972, 1978). An adaptation of the TAS for middle school–aged students, called the *Test Anxiety Scale for Adolescents* (TASA), was developed by Schmitt and Crocker (1982) but has not received wide use. For historical interest, a sample of items from the 37-item TAS is reproduced in Figure 5–1.

Altogether, probably two dozen or more checklists, surveys, questionnaires, and other instruments have been developed to try to quantify test-anxiety levels. A very thorough list, with brief descriptions of 45 instruments designed to measure test anxiety or a related characteristic, has been compiled by Anderson and Sauser (1995).

In this chapter, however, we narrow that number down considerably by applying certain criteria. We wanted to illustrate test-anxiety instruments that would be fairly readily available to most readers, either by mail, through a local college or university library, or by contacting the author or publisher of an instrument by mail or via the Internet. (We wanted to exclude instruments that would cause excessive anxiety to locate or obtain.) We also wanted to limit our illustrations to those instruments that would be most useful for use with elementary and secondary school students.

Second, as specialists in the area of educational measurement, we have some expertise in the characteristics that make up a good test, and

Figure 5–1   Sample Items from the *Test Anxiety Scale*

T	F	1. While taking an important exam, I find myself thinking of how much brighter the other students are than I am. (T)
T	F	2. If I were to take an intelligence test, I would worry a great deal before taking it. (T)
T	F	3. If I knew I was going to take an intelligence test, I would feel confident and relaxed. (F)
T	F	4. While taking an important exam, I perspire a great deal. (T)
T	F	5. During course examinations, I find myself thinking of things unrelated to the actual course material. (T)

NOTES:

1. From Sarason (1972); no directions for students or scoring information are available.

2. Letters in parentheses correspond to answer choices that indicate higher levels of test anxiety and would not appear on the instrument as administered to students.

3. The TAS exists in two forms: a "nervous" version, and a "relaxed" version, which differ only in the wording of the items. For example, an item in the nervous version that asks "Do you worry a lot while taking a test?" would be reworded to "Do you feel relaxed while taking a test?" in the relaxed version. A comparison of the relaxed and nervous items is provided in Harnisch, Hill, and Fyans (1980). The items and scoring keys shown in this figure represent the nervous version, which has been used considerably more often than the relaxed version. Scoring keys for the relaxed version are reversed.

we wanted to apply that knowledge to the task of recommending test-anxiety instruments. Characteristics such as reliability and validity are essential for a test, to obtain dependable results and accurate information about whatever it is they purport to measure. We culled the various available test-anxiety instruments and favored for inclusion here those that tended to have stronger psychometric characteristics.

Third, we did not rely solely on our own judgments or on the claims of test publishers. It might come as a surprise to learn that anyone can develop and sell or promote a test. It is easy to see examples of this on the covers of magazines that proclaim: "Are You and Your Man/Woman Truly Compatible? Take our 5-Minute Love Test!" A quick Internet search for *IQ tests* will confirm that dozens of home-made creations purporting to measure intelligence are available—most with little or no scientific credibility. To save readers from this kind of "assessment alchemy," we favored instruments that have been subjected to a rigorous peer-review process in which the quality of the test and the accuracy of the information it provides have been evaluated by independent specialists.

Finally, some readers may want more information about a particular test-anxiety instrument. And some readers may not want to choose an untested instrument, preferring instead an instrument that has some history of being used and that includes some reliable information about the experiences of others. Unfortunately, only some of the available instruments have documentation to support whatever claims of psychometric quality are made, and some instruments have seen only modest application and therefore have little usage base to help a reader arrive at an informed choice. We wanted to err on the side of including instruments that have both a record and a track record to support their use.

Keeping in mind these criteria, we culled from among the possible test-anxiety instruments those instruments listed in Table 5–1, which gives the title of the instrument; the target group for which the test was designed; a citation for the most recent publication date or edition with source/contact information; and (if available) one or more citations for independent reviews of the instrument.

We recognize that the information provided in Table 5–1 is very limited, but we also sensed that including too much detail on available instruments at this point might be, well, too much detail. However, we know that some readers will want as much detail on the assessment of test anxiety as possible. For those readers, we have included Appendix C. The appendix provides our own summary and review of each of the instruments listed in Table 5–1, as well as information about the process by which tests are evaluated by testing professionals.

Summary

We recognize the irony of the situation. A teacher, school counselor, or other educator suspects that for a student they are concerned about, the specter of taking a test brings on negative thoughts, fears of failure, nervous symptoms, and dread. The last thing that the educator might think of doing is to give the student a test. Indeed, taking a test to measure test anxiety is the last thing the student might want to do!

In this chapter and the related appendix, we tried to accomplish three goals. First, we wanted the reader to know that a number of high-quality instruments are available if it seems desirable to measure the degree of test anxiety in a student or in a group of students. Second, we wanted to be of some help in the process of locating an instrument, by sorting through the various options that exist, and selecting those that met criteria for defensible use and would be likely

Table 5-1 Overview of Test Anxiety Instruments

Title	Target Student Group	Citation and Source/Contact Information	Source for Independent Reviews (if available)
Children's Test Anxiety Scale (CTAS)	Elementary school	Wren, D. G., & Benson, J. (2001, July). *Development and validation of a children's test anxiety scale.* Paper presented at the annual meeting of the Stress and Anxiety Research Society, Palma de Mallorca, Spain.	Not available.
Suinn Test Anxiety Behavior Scale (STABS)	College (though may be appropriate for high school)	Suinn, R. M. (1971a). *Suinn test anxiety behavior scale.* Fort Collins, CO: Rocky Mountain Behavior Science Institute. P.O. Box 1066 Fort Collins, CO 80522	Endler, N. S. (1978). Review of Suinn Test Anxiety Behavior Scale. In O. K. Buros (Ed.), *The eighth mental measurements yearbook* (pp. 1104–1106). Lincoln, NE: University of Nebraska Press.
Test Anxiety Inventory (TAI)	Junior high school, high school, college	Spielberger, C. D. (1977). *Test anxiety inventory.* Palo Alto, CA: Consulting Psychologists Press. Available from: Mind Garden 1690 Woodside Rd., Suite 202 Redwood City, CA 94061 Tel: (650) 261-3500 E-mail: mindgarden@msn.com	Galassi, J. P. (1985b). Review of Test Attitude Inventory. In J. V. Mitchell (Ed.), *The ninth mental measurements yearbook* (pp. 1547–1548). Lincoln, NE: University of Nebraska Press.

(Continued)

Table 5–1 (Continued)

Title	Target Student Group	Citation and Source/Contact Information	Source for Independent Reviews (if available)
Test Anxiety Profile (TAP)	High School, college	Oetting, E. R., & Cole, C. W. (1980). *Test anxiety profile*. Fort Collins, CO: Tri-Ethnic Center for Prevention Research. No longer commercially marketed, but available from: Tri-Ethnic Center for Prevention Research Colorado State University 100 Sage Hall Fort Collins, CO 80523-1879 Tel: (800) 835-8091	Brown, S. D. (1985). Review of Test Anxiety Profile. In J. V. Mitchell (Ed.), *The ninth mental measurements yearbook* (pp. 1543–1545). Lincoln, NE: University of Nebraska Press. Galassi, J. P. (1985a). Review of Test Anxiety Profile. In J. V. Mitchell (Ed.), *The ninth mental measurements yearbook* (pp. 1545–1546). Lincoln, NE: University of Nebraska Press.
FRIEDBEN Test Anxiety Scale	Middle/junior high school	Friedman, I. A., & Bendas-Jacob, O. (1997). Measuring perceived test anxiety in adolescents: A self-report scale. *Educational and Psychological Measurement, 57*(6), 1035–1046. Available from: Professor Isaac A. Firedman, Director The Henrietta Szold Institute 9 Columbia St. Jerusalem, 96583, Israel	Not available.

to give reliable and valid results. Finally, along the way, we wanted to continue to share with readers some important concepts related to testing—concepts that would be helpful both for understanding the test-anxiety instrument critiques we offered and in other situations that are encountered in educational contexts.

In summary, if a teacher wanted to gauge the general level of anxiety about testing in his or her class, or if a school counselor wanted to measure the test-anxiety level of a specific student before and after intervention to alleviate the student's test anxiety, sound instruments are available for those purposes, and promising new instruments are undergoing further validation. The brief, nonthreatening, and linguistically accessible test-anxiety instruments described in this chapter can be used with very young students in elementary school, with high school students, and with older students enrolled in community colleges, GED programs, or universities. Less-sound instruments also exist, and we hope that potential users will steer clear of those.

We recommend of course that anyone who administers an instrument such as we have listed in this chapter or described in Appendix C, or anyone who provides interpretation of the results, be qualified to do so. To that end, we think that the typical college-level course taken by most educators as part of their undergraduate preservice preparation would provide sufficient background. It is possible, too, that the test-anxiety instruments described here could be administered by an appropriate paraprofessional under the supervision of a qualified educator. In any case, users should familiarize themselves with the administration and interpretation guidelines provided by the publisher of an instrument and should possess whatever qualifications the test-maker requires.

If there is any doubt about whether a person should be involved in administering, scoring, or interpreting the results of a test-anxiety instrument, it would be best to review relevant professional testing guidelines, such as those found in the *Code of Fair Testing Practices* (Joint Committee on Testing Practices, 2004), which serves as "a guide for professionals in fulfilling their obligation to provide and use tests that are fair to all test takers regardless of age, gender, disability, race, ethnicity, national origin, religion, sexual orientation, linguistic background, or other personal characteristics" (p. 1). Similar guidelines and information can be found in the *Rights and Responsibilities of Test Takers* (Joint Committee on Testing Practices, 2000) or the *Code of Professional Responsibilities in Educational Measurement* (National Council on Measurement in Education, 1995). Additional information about these resources can be found in Appendix B.

Of course, it is not necessary to administer a test-anxiety instrument to any student. An attentive and concerned educator might well recognize that one or more students in a class manifests symptoms of debilitating test anxiety. For those students, simple interventions can be implemented to provide assistance. Indeed, with the increase in the frequency of tests and the consequences associated with testing, it is likely interventions provided at a broader level (e.g., in the classroom) would be helpful for many students. Answering the question, "What can be done about test anxiety?" is the focus of the next chapter.

6

Tips and Strategies for Reducing Test Anxiety

Four-letter words can evoke strong emotions or reactions. *Fire. Love. Diet. Kill.*

We suspect that the four-letter words that are the topic of this book—words like *test, exam, quiz,* and *fear*—have similar evocative potential.

However, the specific question we address in this chapter is, "What can be done to address test anxiety in the high-stakes contexts in which it is now so often observed?" Our answer is, *lots* . . . and in this chapter we will try to offer *hope*.

Despite test anxiety's prevalence and effects, there are remedies, strategies, and preventive measures that can be employed to minimize its influence. Most of these methods can be easily implemented by students, teachers, and parents. To begin this chapter, we will first provide a nontechnical overview of the theory and research that supports strategies for test-anxiety reduction. Then we will provide a concrete list of practical techniques and strategies for reducing test anxiety.

Stop the Ride, I Want to Get Off!

It's a vicious cycle. Test anxiety leads to poor test performance. Accurate test performance is hindered by rising levels of test anxiety. And so on and so on. But what is known about breaking the cycle? As we have seen in the previous chapters, test anxiety is a multifaceted phenomenon. Reducing test anxiety requires a multifaceted approach. We cannot say that research has discovered a miracle pill or a simple solution to cure test anxiety, but we can offer some suggestions about how to proceed—and how not to.

Theoretically, interventions for reducing test anxiety can be grouped into five categories: (a) behavioral, (b) cognitive, (c) cognitive-behavioral, (d) study skills, and (e) test-taking skills. Table 6–1 provides a listing of the five categories, along with a description of the focus of each type of intervention. For example, cognitive treatments address the worry aspect of test anxiety. The table also includes examples of treatments and research findings.

The most effective interventions for test anxiety appear to be combinations of cognitive and behavioral treatments with skill-focused approaches (Ergene, 2003; Hembree, 1988). Both anxiety components—worry and emotionality—need to be addressed as part of an effective intervention. However, research has demonstrated that it is the addition of skill-focused interventions—that is, adequate academic preparation—that provides a total approach to addressing the problem. And, researchers have found that the test-anxiety–reducing effects of these combination interventions have fairly long lives; that is, their beneficial effects for students do not appear to decline appreciably over time.

Before leaving the theoretical realm, there is a final consideration that should be mentioned. (Actually, it's more like the elephant in the room that everyone notices but no one talks about.) Reducing test anxiety may or may not increase a student's test scores or grades; at least, any increase may not be immediately observed. The reasons for this are twofold. First, there are many factors besides test anxiety that contribute to a student's test performance. Reducing test anxiety may indeed help to obtain a truer and more accurate picture of a student's knowledge, skills, and abilities, but we must hasten to highlight that we said "truer and more accurate," which does not necessarily mean "higher." Second, other factors contribute to test performance, and the effects of test anxiety reach beyond just the tests. Frustration, fear, and low motivation may interfere with attempts by students to learn new materials and skills. This means

Table 6–1   Overview of Interventions for Test Anxiety and Research Results

Intervention Type	Focus of Intervention	Examples of Intervention	Research Findings
Behavioral	Emotionality (however, treatment effects aid in worry reduction as well)	*Relaxation techniques *Hypnosis *Systematic desensitization *Covert positive reinforcement	All result in TA reduction; also increase facilitative TA
Cognitive	Worry	*Modify or eliminate thought patterns contributing to symptoms	Not effective in reducing TA
Cognitive-behavioral	Combination of worry and emotionality	*Anxiety-management training *Attentional training *Cognitive modification *Stress inoculation	All associated with higher levels of facilitative TA
Study Skills	Knowledge/skills deficit	*Advance organizers/ previewing *Frequent review and practice *Time managment	Not effective (alone) in reducing TA
Test-Taking Skills	Poor test-taking skills	*Test-taking strategies (e.g., time management, informed guessing, etc.)	Results in moderate reduction in TA for students with low test-taking skills

that, although a poor-performing student may require additional review and enhanced instruction in key course content and objectives, the good news is that the removal of the interference presented by test anxiety can facilitate such learning.

Practical Strategies and Techniques for Addressing Test Anxiety

What can students, teachers, administrators, and parents do to help reduce test anxiety? Within that question lies the key to effectively addressing the problem—students, teachers, administrators, and parents are all necessary to the process of successfully reducing test anxiety. Each one has responsibilities and roles; Table 6–2 presents an overview of how each can actively participate in the process. The table is formatted so that a check mark ☑ at the intersection of any particular row and column indicates a primary responsibility. For example, the first check mark in Row 1 (Structure of Lessons) means that teachers and administrators have primary control and responsibility for this kind of intervention. Of course, some methods require cooperation among several groups. For example, the check marks in Row 11 (Study Skills) indicate that students must put forth effort to acquire these skills and that parents and teachers must work with students to teach, reinforce, and practice them. Even suggestions that may only be checked for one group will, in reality, likely require at least some overlapping effort on the part of others. In the sections that follow, we describe each of the areas and specific intervention strategies in detail.

Classrooms and Schools

Most testing takes place in the classroom, so the classroom is a logical first avenue to consider as a context for intervention. We must hasten to admit our familiarity with the demands of teaching. It is clearly a complicated, demanding job that is difficult to do well. The rewards are great, but there are certainly many challenges along the way. By first addressing the category of classrooms and schools, we do not want to be seen as piling another burden on educators to "fix" something. Rather, the following suggestions are intended to help kill two birds with one stone, to refine or modify existing practices in ways that help educators help students even more.

Structure of Lessons

Test anxiety appears to be lower in classrooms where more opportunities for previewing and reviewing are integrated into the classroom (Berliner & Casanova, 1988; Helmke, 1988; Wilkinson, 1990). When behavioral objectives were popular pedagogy in the 1970s, many teachers were taught to write the lesson objective on the

Table 6–2   Strategies for Reducing Test Anxiety

Focus Area	*Requires active involvement of . . .*		
Reduction Technique	*Students*	*Teachers/ Administrators/ School Counselors*	*Parents*
Classrooms and Schools			
1. Structure of lessons		☑	
2. Classroom atmosphere		☑	
3. Assessment environment		☑	☑
4. Assessment techniques		☑	
5. Assessment setting		☑	
6. Test preparation	☑	☑	☑
Family Life Factors			
7. Home environment			☑
8. Parental expectations			☑
Student-Centered Approaches			
9. Self-talk	☑		
10. Relaxation techniques	☑		
11. Study skills	☑	☑	☑
Communication Patterns			
12. Attitudes, beliefs, and perceptions	☑	☑	☑
13. Use of competition		☑	☑
14. Praise construction		☑	☑
15. Assessment literacy		☑	☑
16. Review scores, tests, and work	☑	☑	☑

board; for example, "Today's lesson: solve two-step equations." (Notice the use of the action word *solve*.) However, what we are referring to here is different. We are talking about helping students create a bigger picture of what they are learning and how it fits together, similar to the concept of an advance organizer. It's about using opportunities to review, rather than setting aside separate time "to review." For example, teaching a lesson about reflecting points over the *x*-axis (where the *y*-coordinate changes sign) also presents a great opportunity for reviewing the rules about multiplying negative numbers. Previewing and reviewing can help move students toward a deeper conceptual understanding of the material and to develop **metacognition** skills, which have been shown to increase motivation, memory of materials, and flexible knowledge (Carpenter & Lehrer, 1999).

Another strategy relates to the research finding that test anxiety appears to be higher in students whose teachers are highly efficient with classroom time (Berliner & Casanova, 1988; Helmke, 1988). It turns out that being *too* efficient can be related to increased student anxiety. At first, this finding may seem counterintuitive. However, large volumes of new material can seem overwhelming and can create anxiety for some students. A balance is needed, to blend curriculum coverage with instructional density (i.e., taking time for things like talking and working individually with students, or encouraging reflection). This is no small feat—another example of what makes teaching so difficult—but some trade-off in efficiency may result in less anxiety for students related to their performance and more accurate assessment information.

Classroom Atmosphere

The emphasis on evaluation in the classroom also can generate pressure on students. If the focus of the classroom is on testing, then the worry about tests is increased. The debilitating effects of test anxiety are accentuated in classrooms where teachers, classmates, and peers pressure students to do well. It is clear that some motivation to do well is appropriate, and we know that schoolwide programs (e.g., awards, pep assemblies) designed to get students pumped up to perform well on tests are well intentioned.

However, other researchers worry that "school programs designed to increase motivation to perform on tests and parental pressure to perform well may backfire if they produce heightened anxiety" (Wolf & Smith, 1993, p. 39). In one study, researchers found noticeable differences in the levels of stress in the schools they studied, which they hypothesized may have been attributable to the differential emphasis the principals of those schools placed on raising test scores (Fleege et al., 1992). Greater stress levels were exhibited in the schools where teachers were urged during faculty meetings to practice testlike activities with their students or when teachers were reminded of the use of test scores by the public to gauge the success of the school. Anxiety also was higher at schools where students were encouraged during morning and afternoon announcements over the school's public address system to do their best on the upcoming test, or when students were reminded of the importance of getting a good night's rest, eating a good breakfast, and so on.

We suggest that teachers, principals, and other educators must work to establish nonthreatening school and classroom environments in which the goal is more evidently learning than test results or grades. This is, of course, easier said than done, and we suspect that some readers—especially teachers and administrators under accountability systems—may be saying, "But you don't know the pressure we are under to get high scores!" True enough: high-stakes testing and accountability and the concomitant stresses that often accompany them are probably here to stay. However, educators must be on particular guard against passing along to students their anxieties about testing. The best strategy is to communicate to students that testing is important and is to be taken seriously, but not to transmit undue pressures.

Assessment Environment

The assessment culture in a classroom is a special part of the overall classroom atmosphere and is particularly important in addressing test anxiety. A healthy assessment environment is one in which the role, types, characteristics, purposes, and consequences of testing are clearly and openly presented and discussed with students and parents.

We assume that nearly all readers of this book have had some assessment experiences that were unpleasant or that were not examples of good assessment practice. For example, it is almost certain that our readers' own educational backgrounds include exposure to instances of poorly written tests, trick questions, uncertainty about what a test would cover, tests that were not good representations of the material that had been covered, grading systems that were unfair, and so on. To reduce test-related anxiety, a healthy assessment environment—that is, one in which testing is a natural, transparent, and professional part of the learning process—should be established and maintained.

A list of eight characteristics of a healthy assessment environment is provided in Table 6–3. For example, the first characteristic listed in Table 6–3 indicates that those who give tests should provide test takers with relevant information about evaluations that would have the potential to induce anxiety. Students should be informed, at the beginning of the year and as often as seems appropriate during the year, about the type, number, point or grade value, and dates of tests,

Table 6–3   Strategies for Promoting a Healthy Assessment Environment

1. *Provide basic information about evaluations.* Inform students at the beginning of the year (and provide friendly reminders) of the type, frequency, value, and dates of tests, assignments, and other evaluation components that will count toward their grades.

2. *Be fair and open about testing.* In advance of any test that will count toward a grade, provide students with adequate notice and a concrete description of the content, length, format, timing, guidelines, and/or other requirements for completing the test (i.e., test specifications).

3. *Be fair and open about graded assignments.* For written assignments that will count toward a grade, provide, in advance, a scoring rubric or evaluation framework that details requirements for the written assignment, such as topic be covered, the order of required elements, style, resources to be used, specific subheadings, and so on, and information about the grading scale that will be used.

4. *Consider other pressures on students.* To the extent possible, avoid scheduling examinations or due dates for major papers concurrently with other important assignments or examinations or at other times during which the student may have additional responsibilities or commitments outside the classroom (e.g., family vacation times, holidays, school dance, or sporting event).

5. *Limit the number of tests and assignments that count toward a grade.* Not every quiz or assignment needs to receive a grade; many can be completed for formative or purely instructional purposes. Stiggins (2005) refers to this as "assessment *for* learning."

6. *Don't assess what you don't intend to assess.* For example, a timed test (also known as a speeded test) might be appropriate if a teacher were interested in assessing students' speed of response or ability to work under pressure. If those characteristics are not what is intended to be assessed—but the intention is to measure content knowledge, understanding, or skills only—then a speeded test would not be appropriate. The opposite of a speeded test (called a power test) means allowing sufficient time for students to complete the test, and the assurance and experience of sufficient time helps allay testing anxieties.

7. *Use grades only as indicators of achievement.* Using grades punitively can heighten anxiety about evaluation. For example, do not lower an achievement grade because of poor attendance. Avoid grading on the curve, which takes control of achievement out of the hands of a student—inducing anxiety—and makes a student's grade dependent on how other students perform.

8. *Foster balanced perspectives about assessment.* Create, describe to students, and foster an assessment climate in which students see grades not only as indicators of achievement but also as valuable indicators of their strengths and weaknesses.

assignments, and other evaluation components that will count toward their grades.

Assessment Techniques

Using multiple evaluation practices and formats is advantageous for several reasons. For example, teachers should consider not relying exclusively on oral presentations, performances, or multiple-choice tests, but should include a mix of these, as appropriate to the curriculum goals and objectives being assessed. Some students tend to perform better and to have greater self-confidence and comfort with some formats over others. Reliance on a single type of assessment technique puts some students at a disadvantage, induces test anxiety for those students, and results in less-accurate measures of their true knowledge, skill, or ability. Obviously, it is desirable, to the greatest extent possible, to obtain test scores for students that are more reflective of their achievement than of their affinity for a particular assessment format. Teachers can minimize effects of the test format and can obtain more accurate information about student achievement by using a variety of assessment techniques. An ancillary benefit of this practice is that it exposes students to a wider variety of formats, and such familiarity is likely to be beneficial to them in other testing situations in the future.

One assessment technique that should be avoided is the "pop" or surprise test. Although the rationale for this practice is clear and laudable (namely, to promote frequent review and good study habits), the effects are clearly harmful for some students. Brief, frequent, announced quizzes can promote the same goals without the corresponding anxiety-producing effects. Indeed, we actually recommend more testing, in general, as an additional and effective way to help students deal with test anxiety. A series of several brief, well-constructed, and clearly described-in-advance tests (see the guidelines in Table 6–3) that constitute a smaller percentage of an overall grade are much more likely to be educationally effective and to produce less anxiety than a few longer, poorly constructed, surprise tests, or tests that compose a major portion of a final grade. Research has shown, too, that fewer, less-weighty examinations reduce the effects of anxiety on students. In one such study, students given weekly tests showed less test anxiety, less task-irrelevant behavior during testing, and better performance than students who were given only a midterm examination (Sumprer & Hollandsworth, 1982).

It is not only the test questions themselves that can induce debilitating test anxiety; other, related features of a test can produce this effect.

For example, as we saw in Chapter 5, some versions of instruments designed to measure test anxiety purposefully omit reference to anxiety in the title of the instrument administered to students, in order to prevent inducing additional anxiety. The same principle can be extended to classroom assessment situations in which teachers who create tests can also create or communicate directions for the test that induce more or less anxiety. One early study of the effect of test directions compared a standard set of directions to one that was meant to reassure test-anxious students. Students in the standard condition were told that they would be shown a series of words and would be required to recall as many words as they could. Because the words would be shown in rapid succession, several attempts would be permitted. Students in the reassurance condition were, in addition, told the following:

> Before we start, perhaps I should mention a few things that will be helpful to you in learning the list I am going to show you. . . . Many people get unduly upset and tense because they do not learn the list in just a few trials. If you don't worry about how you are doing, but rather just concentrate on the list, you will find you learn much more easily. These kinds of lists are hard, and so it's no surprise or matter of concern if you progress slowly at first and make mistakes. (Sarason, 1958, p. 473)

Highly test-anxious students who were provided with the additional, reassuring directions performed better than a comparison group of highly anxious students who received only the standard directions. (Interestingly, students who were very low in anxiety to begin with actually performed worse when given the reassurance.) In general, however, it would seem appropriate to recommend that teachers provide test directions that at least do not heighten anxiety, and possibly that they provide directions that put students at ease. Some researchers have even suggested that, in a very few situations, the effect of test anxiety can be moderated by grouping students of different anxiety levels and providing the groups with different versions of the test instructions (Hembree, 1988).

Finally, recent research suggests that, for some tests, educators might consider permitting students to work in groups of two or more to complete the test. We (the authors) would not want the ophthalmologist who performs a delicate eye surgery on us to have passed his or her board examination with the assistance of a friend! Indeed, there are many situations, even in elementary school classrooms, in which an educator has the legitimate purpose of obtaining accurate information about the independent level of knowledge, skill, or ability of a particular student. However, it is just as clear that not all assessments need to have that purpose. Many assessments can serve the dual aims of evaluation and instruction; some assessments may even have the primary goal of being a learning experience for students (for a description, see Chappuis & Stiggins, 2002; Stiggins, 2005).

Similar to cooperative learning, a new approach—cooperative testing—has been tried and found to be highly successful in preliminary studies. In one study, researchers created three kinds of testing conditions for 576 college-level psychology students (Zimbardo, Butler, & Wolfe, 2003). One group of students was assigned to testing teams; a second group of students was allowed to choose a teammate to take a test with; the third group of students was assigned to take the test in the traditional (i.e., solo) fashion. The researchers found that both of the team conditions produced achievement results that were significantly higher than the solo condition. (For those who recall our discussion of effect size, the effect size in this case was huge: ES = .80.) In addition to greater achievement, students in the cooperative conditions also reported increased self-confidence, less cheating, increased enjoyment of the subject matter, and reduced levels of test anxiety.

To achieve a reduction in test anxiety, it is apparently helpful even if students merely study with a teammate or are permitted to express themselves during a test. In one study, when a student prepared for an upcoming test together with a supportive friend or classmate, test anxiety was reduced (Sarason, 1981). In another study, students with high levels of test anxiety who were given the chance to write comments on a test concerning the questions in the test performed better than similar students who were not given the same opportunity (Davis, 1993).

Assessment Setting

The physical setting for a test—the lighting, the temperature, and the working space—needs to be considered and adjusted so that students feel less anxious, are more secure and comfortable, and can focus better on the task at hand. Although there is no strong evidence to recommend the practice, there is at least some urban legend that suggests playing classical music lowers anxiety levels and improves students' test performance.

Whether or not it turns out that music is beneficial, there is abundant evidence that other factors about the assessment setting make a difference. The environment should provide adequate space for working on the test; it should be well lighted, should have appropriate temperature control, and should be free of distractions. A conducive assessment setting is one that accommodates characteristics of the students (e.g., appropriate facilities for left- and right-handed students or for students with special physical needs such as visual, auditory, or motor impairments). Although this is not often considered, we have observed the difficulty and discomfort of particularly large-framed or overweight students, when appropriate seating is not provided for them.

As teachers ourselves, we have had many opportunities to arrange an assessment environment so that it was amenable to students demonstrating their true level of knowledge or skill on an examination, without the interference of test anxiety. One of us (GJC) had a memorable experience that might illustrate the extent to which simple changes in the assessment setting can be helpful.

Prior to a final examination in a testing and measurements course at the college level, a woman (who we will call Emily) approached me (the instructor) and wanted to know what her final grade would be if she skipped the final examination. After some probing, I learned that Emily was terrified of examinations and that she would rather take a lower grade than be subjected to the terror of an examination. She explained that the time limit, the dreaded silence in the examination room, having to sit in a desk for two hours, and other factors caused her to become gripped with fear, freeze up, and become unable to complete a test. Based on the quality of her in-class comments and homework assignments, I judged Emily to be a very capable student. I asked her how she prepared for class meetings, did her assignments, and so forth. She explained that she usually did so at home, on the floor of her room. She wore sweatpants or pajamas, she listened to music, she had all of her materials (and lots of snacks) spread out on the floor around her.

As the instructor—and as a measurement specialist—my primary concern for the final examination was that I would obtain a fair and accurate indication of Emily's mastery of the content covered by the final, and that every student took the final under essentially the same, secure conditions so that scores could be meaningfully compared. I asked Emily if, instead of skipping the final examination, she would be willing to take it under conditions that would be more like the conditions in which she prepared for class. We were able to arrange a secure conference room for her to take the final examination, with the only modification to the room being that the clock on the wall was removed. A graduate assistant proctored the exam by ensuring that Emily only took into the conference room materials that were permissible for the final exam and by informing her when the two-hour time limit had elapsed. Of course, the permissible materials for Emily included her CD player and some CDs, an assortment of snack food, and the test. Dressed in her sweats and with the final examination spread out on the floor of the conference room, Emily did just fine.

Test Preparation

Test anxiety is reduced when a student feels adequately prepared for a test. Obviously, this includes attainment of whatever curriculum goals, **content standards**, or skills that the test is designed to measure. Of all the strategies for reducing test anxiety, the surest and most effective is when a student possesses a justifiable confidence that he or she has, prior to testing, achieved mastery of whatever content or skills a test will cover. Becker (1982) has demonstrated that what is called **overlearning**—that is, repeated review and practice to the point of automaticity—constitutes, as the FDA might say, a safe and effective preventative for test anxiety.

In addition, however, preparation for taking a test should include familiarity with the parameters of the test and acquisition of test-taking skills. It is first important to familiarize students with what the test will actually look like, how long it will be, how many questions it will have, what topics will be covered, how much time will be permitted, how answers will need to be recorded, what kinds of response formats are permitted (e.g., outlining, complete sentences, or show your work), and other parameters of the test. If, for example, it is known that the state-mandated writing test will require students to read a short poem and then respond to that prompt with a three-paragraph persuasive essay defending or rejecting the author's use of controversial language in the poem, then the day of the test is not the first time students should be writing such an essay. In that situation, it is appropriate test preparation to familiarize students with writing short, persuasive essays in response to various kinds of prompts.

Instruction and assessment should be purposefully aligned not only to allay testing anxiety but also because such alignment is an important piece of validity evidence for the assessment. It is a general rule of good teaching and testing that students should be provided with practice on whatever content will be tested and the methods by which it will be assessed. Indeed, if some knowledge, skill, or objective is found in the relevant state content standards, and if those content standards are assessed, then *not* teaching it would be professionally indefensible.

Students also can benefit from explicit instruction in other test-taking skills. For example, students should know how to manage the time allotted to complete a test. They should learn how to pace themselves during a test and when to move on to another task if they become bogged down. They should know whether there is a penalty for guessing on multiple-choice items or it is to their advantage to answer all items, making informed guesses when they are unsure. Students should also receive direct instruction in how to read, interpret, and follow the directions of a test. A student may write an outstanding essay for a state-mandated writing test, but if the essay does not squarely address the topic, or if it fails to include the characteristics specified in the directions, then the standard scoring rubric applied to the essays will not reward the student's work. Readers interested in materials for teaching test-taking skills are referred to the work of Moke and Shermis (2001), whose *Success with Test-Taking* resource is described in Appendix B.

Although we strongly recommend test preparation and that students acquire test-taking skills, some test-preparation activities can cross a line of ethical practice. For example, a colleague in educational testing tells the story of a principal who began the announcements each morning by greeting the students over the school's public address system: "Good morning students, and salutations! Do you know what a salutation is? It means *greeting*, like the greeting you see at the beginning of a letter." Although many students who listened to that announcement learned the meaning of words like *salutation* from the principal's daily announcements, they probably never learned that his choice of words wasn't random but instead was drawn from the vocabulary subtest of the state-mandated, norm-referenced test.

As we have noted previously, some schools may set aside some time before an important test administration to begin preparing students to take the tests, or to enhance student motivation to do well on them via pep rallies, and so on. In our home state of North Carolina, important tests called End-of-Grade tests (EOGs) are a feature of the state accountability system. One of the authors of this book observed bulletin boards in the hallway of a school that were emblazoned, "We are in training for the EOGs!", complete with copies of sample bubble sheets and photocopies of test-booklet covers. The bulletin boards reminded teachers and students alike of the goal: doing well on the EOGs.

Certainly, it is appropriate to inform students about approaching, consequential tests. And it is probably even a good idea for students to be familiar with what the test materials will look like. We urge caution in two respects, however. First, such displays and focus on high-stakes testing may actually heighten anxiety for some teachers and students as they prepare for "the big one." Rather than implementing a monumental test-preparation campaign just prior to a test, a better strategy would be to subtly integrate modest test-preparation activities into the curriculum and to distribute exposure to appropriate, educationally relevant test-taking skills more evenly throughout the school year.

Second, it is important to distinguish between ethical and unethical test-preparation activities. As has been described elsewhere (see Cizek, 2001a, 2003b, 2003c), accountability pressures have been accompanied by an increase in the incidence of unethical test-preparation activities and of cheating on the part of students, teachers, administrators, and parents.

Sometimes the line between ethical and unethical test preparation is blurry. However, some guidance is available, and a number of testing specialists have weighed in on the topic. Table 6–4 provides a list of test-preparation activities drawn from the work of several specialists (Haladyna, Nolen, & Haas, 1991; Mehrens, 1991; Mehrens & Kaminski, 1989). The list is organized as a continuum, ranging from activities posing little or no ethical concern to those which almost surely breach professional ethics of both teaching and testing. Although individual circumstances and professional judgment of specific activities will vary, the table should provide a guide for considering test-preparation activities to avoid. Finally, whereas the authors frame their guidelines in the context of preparing students for performance assessments, Mehrens, Popham, and Ryan (1998) list six general principles that can be applied broadly to diverse assessment contexts and that provide guidelines for helping educators to distinguish appropriate from inappropriate test-preparation activities.

Family Life Factors

Some readers may be familiar with the new slogan used in the federal government's campaign to fight drug use: "Parents. The Anti-Drug." Analogously, because the root causes of test anxiety are thought to lie in early childhood experiences and parental expectations, we think a similar slogan captures the importance of family life factors: "Parents. The Anti-Anxiety Treatment." Research on this

Table 6–4   Continuum of Test-Preparation Activities

Test-Preparation Activity	*Ethical Continuum*
Teaching students general test-taking skills	Most Ethical
Checking students' answer sheets to verify that they been properly completed	
Attempting to increasing student motivation to perform on the test (e.g., through appeals to parents, students, educators)	
Teaching the objectives covered by a test	
Assessing students *only* via the format used on a test	
Developing a curriculum based on the content of the test	
Using score-boosting materials based on a current form of test	
Teaching *only* objectives covered by a test	
Using items similar to those on a test for instructional purposes	
Teaching *only* the specific task covered by a performance assessment	
Discouraging weaker students from participating in a test	
Using secure items from a test for review or practice	Highly Unethical

SOURCE: Adapted from Haladyna, Nolen, and Haas (1991), Mehrens (1991); and Mehrens and Kaminski (1989)

topic reveals that parents are very influential in the development of test anxiety and must figure prominently in its prevention. The following sections on home environment, parental expectations, and family relationships expand on these family-related influences on test anxiety.

Home Environment

The total family environment (e.g., parenting style, quality of communication, encouragement of personal growth, and family relationships) has also been found to be inversely related to children's test-anxiety and trait-anxiety levels. For example, as we cited in

Key Idea #16   Teachers Can Help Head Off Student Test Anxiety By . . .

- including a high degree of explicit structure in lessons;
- de-emphasizing competition and grade orientation;
- creating and maintaining a safe and comfortable assessment environment;
- using diverse assessment techniques;
- providing ample opportunities and help for students preparing for tests; and
- ensuring that appropriate test-administration accommodations are made for students who need them.

Chapter 3, adolescent children of divorced parents tend to have higher levels of test anxiety than do children of intact families (Guttman, 1987). In a study by Peleg-Popko and Klingman (2002), the authors found that boys' levels of test anxiety were negatively related to the encouragement of personal growth they received from parents, whereas no such relationship was found for girls. Such an observation suggests that cultural family-rearing phenomena are at work. The fact that boys who receive less personal-growth support tend to report lower levels of test anxiety is perhaps a reflection of cultural and family structures in which boys are expected and encouraged to be independent and to express themselves, whereas girls are expected to conform to family rules and demands. The resulting higher levels of autonomy in boys may also help reduce their levels of anxiety. The same independence-facilitating environments may foster autonomy and reduced anxiety for girls.

In another study, researchers found that "parental child rearing techniques are related to [test-anxiety] development in children" in the following way:

> Failure of a parent to provide emotional support to a child while in a problem solving situation and the failure to reinforce an internal locus of evaluation can result in lower achievement scores and a child who is not task-oriented. If this cycle continues, as a child gets older, there is a greater reliance on external evaluation of one's performance. This leads to greater levels of anxiety and stress. (Dusek, 1980, cited in Sapp, 1999, p. 272)

Overall, the presence of positive parent-child relationships increases the probability of successful academic performances while minimizing the potential for debilitating levels of test anxiety. Thus, in conclusion, we concur with experts in family studies who recommend that prevention of test anxiety should include "encouraging parents and their children to improve their family environment, possibly by providing them with a variety of better communication skills and strategies" (Peleg-Popko & Klingman, 2002, p. 462).

Parental Expectations

"The origins of test anxiety are believed by some to lie in the academic expectations parents place on their children" (McDonald, 2001, p. 91). Some theorists even believe that test anxiety emerges in children as young as preschool-age or during the early elementary school years. It is during these formative years that parents can transmit overly high or unrealistic expectations of their children's performance; eventually, because such expectations cannot always be met, they can create anxiety in children who are fearful of failing to meet them.

Parental expectations and the frequency of testing grow in tandem as children progress through the educational system. As expectations become internalized and testing pressures increase, children, who are also becoming better judges of their own abilities and performances, can experience increasing levels of anxiety centered around testing and evaluative events (Hill & Wigfield, 1984). One study demonstrated that, even in situations in which parents are trying to communicate understanding, encouragement, or interest (e.g., suggesting an earlier bedtime the night before a test or inquiring how a child did on a test), those actions often appear to have the opposite effect (Fleege et al., 1992) by conveying primarily the *importance* of a test. To prevent test anxiety from gaining a foothold during the child's early years, we recommend that parents consider helping children to develop a healthy sense of self-esteem, self-concept, and self-worth by encouraging them, by not overemphasizing the importance of tests, and by establishing rigorous but reasonable standards and reachable expectations.

Student-Centered Approaches

Parents and educators can do much to prevent and to provide effective interventions for test anxiety. However, students themselves can play a critical role in the effort. As can be seen in Table 6–2, students are involved—directly or indirectly—with many of the other techniques listed there. In the following sections, we provide brief descriptions of some of the student-centered techniques that have been shown to be helpful for students in reducing their own levels of test anxiety.

Self-Talk

Self-talk refers to those messages we play over and over in our minds. For anxious students, these messages are often negative ones that can become self-fulfilling prophecies. One effective strategy for reducing test anxiety is for students to learn to replace negative self-talk with positive. To begin with, students should be encouraged to avoid dwelling on what might have happened, what they should have done, and so on. Such cognitions can cause extreme tension and place great demands on the self. Also, students should be advised to avoid "must" self-talk. There is a huge difference between saying, "I want to do well on this test" and "I must do well on this test" (Wilkinson, 1990). Parents and teachers can help with this self-talk reorientation by modeling more positive statements and by encouraging students to replace negative statements with less demanding ones. It is also helpful to suggest that students replace negative thoughts such as "I know I'll blow this test" with more positive self-talk messages, such as "There's a good chance I may do well; even if I don't, it doesn't mean I'm stupid. I can just try harder next time."

Another possible intervention technique that can help reorient self-talk is for teachers (or parents or fellow students) to question students about worst-case scenarios (although this must be done with great care, to avoid the potential that it might inadvertently cause the student to dwell on a negative outcome). For some students, it can be reassuring to discuss the worst thing that can happen in a given situation. For example, a student might consider the question: "Suppose that you do get an F on this test; what would be the worst thing that would result from that?" Especially for younger students, sometimes helping them to apprehend the bigger picture can alleviate irrational or unrealistic fears. Of course, changing one's thinking and self-talk habits is not easy or quickly learned; these techniques must be practiced and reinforced over (at least) several weeks.

Relaxation Techniques

In contrast to other strategies for preventing test anxiety in advance of a test, relaxation techniques can help students cope during a test. Deep breathing helps to relax the muscles in the body and can help students to feel more in control of an event that they might perceive to be out of their control. Alternately tensing and relaxing muscles and muscle groups also can help alleviate some stress during test-taking situations. School counselors or others who may want specific information on how to teach relaxation techniques to individual students are referred to Sapp (1999, pp. 338–351), who provides several pages of scripts for use by trained counselors to help students acquire relaxation skills.

Students may also have other relaxation techniques already at their disposal. Methods for addressing stress, such as meditation, thinking positive thoughts, or recalling peaceful memories, can help reduce anxiety during testing. And the humorous but true axiom applies here: as long as there are tests, there will always be prayer in schools!

Study Skills

As we have mentioned repeatedly, for reducing test anxiety, the importance of adequate studying and understanding of the test material cannot be overstated. Students may need reminders to engage in systematic and regular study and review, and to avoid counterproductive behaviors such as cramming and staying up late the night before a test. Although teachers and parents can work with students to develop effective time management, organization, note-taking skills, and study habits, the responsibility and discipline required to internalize these behaviors ultimately rests with the student. We recommend that students be provided with a simple checklist to help them monitor their own study habits, and that students use the buddy system, teaming up for regular study with a friend so that some accountability and structure is introduced from the beginning. For students with extremely poor study skills, or for whom less intensive strategies are ineffective, Sapp (1999, pp. 328–334) is a source of details on more-focused interventions designed for individual implementation by school counselors or school psychologists.

Communication Patterns

Communication is a powerful tool for good or for ill. We recall a Biblical analogy in which the tongue is compared to the rudder of a ship—a small member with the power to change the course of

---

Key Idea #17   Taming Test Anxiety Before a Test

Students can reduce test anxiety by . . .

learning and practicing test-taking skills;

getting as much information about the upcoming test as possible (e.g., length, time limit, penalty for guessing);

overlearning material to be covered by the test (review, review, review!);

becoming comfortable with any equipment to be used during the test (e.g., calculator, computer, word processing software, lab equipment);

gathering necessary materials for test taking (e.g., pencils, scratch paper, calculator);

learning to recognize the symptoms of test anxiety; and

thinking positive thoughts or anticipating a positive outcome.

---

mammoth vessels. Along those lines, the effect of communication patterns involved in test anxiety is significant. And because the most powerful messages can often be those that are transmitted without using words, we extend our concern to nonverbal communications.

Attitudes, Beliefs, and Perceptions

Children acquire many of their attitudes, beliefs, and perceptions from influential persons in their lives—peers, parents, other family members, and clergy, to name a few. Of course, the list of influences cannot exclude teachers, for whom the job of teaching explicitly entails transmission of values and serving as a model of appropriate conduct.

Obviously, children do not only acquire noble values or observe positive models. If a parent or teacher is anxious about tests, is openly critical of testing, or lacks confidence in his or her assessment acumen, those attitudes and dispositions can affect students' perceptions. For example, one of the authors (SSB) was recently told by a teacher that she purposefully refers to the mandated tests in her state as "the stupid tests" in an attempt to lessen students' worries about the upcoming test administration. Unfortunately, in her well-intentioned

---

O━🗝   **Key Idea #18   Taming Test Anxiety During a Test**

Students can reduce test anxiety by . . .

skimming the entire test first;

building confidence by answering easier questions first, skipping over and then returning to more difficult questions;

keeping track of time limits (if any) and pacing accordingly;

using relaxation techniques (e.g., rest breaks, pauses, relaxation breathing, muscle stretching, rolling the head and neck, arching back and shoulders);

using positive self-talk; and

using learned calming strategies (e.g., meditation, recalling peaceful memories, prayer).

---

attempt to provide comfort and encouragement to test-anxious students, her message is likely to have had the opposite effect. If the tests are indeed stupid, then students would justifiably be unmotivated to perform as well as they can. Worse, if the so-called stupid test turns out to be challenging for a student, self-doubt and anxiety about performance are almost certain to result.

Whether intended or unintended, it is important to avoid communicating to students that tests should be dismissed or considered trifling. Research has shown that

> students have more positive responses to the evaluation process if they perceive that process to address important issues and specific information. Support of the testing process is further increased if the student perceives the process to be reliable and based on sound principle. (Matriello & Dornbush, 1985, cited in Eschemann, 1992, p. 30)

If parents and educators provide students with accurate information about tests and about how the results will be used, students generally will be supportive, motivated, and more interested in the process.

We hasten to add that we are not taking the stance that a teacher's or parent's opposition to state-mandated testing is inappropriate. On the contrary, we strongly support teachers and parents—indeed, all citizens—becoming involved to make positive changes in the educational system wherever they are needed. Parents and educators are vital resources if policymakers are to craft sensible testing policies at the state or local level. Or, if working to influence policy decisions is not possible, then we strongly encourage readers to consider becoming involved with the test-development process. Both authors of this book have had experience working for state testing programs. We know firsthand that such programs are always in need of teachers and parents to serve on oversight panels that help design and critique testing programs, on content standards committees to help circumscribe the depth and breadth of material that forms the basis for tests in each grade and subject area, on review committees to help screen out potentially biased or inappropriate test items or tasks, and even on panels charged with creating the test items and tasks themselves.

Use of Competition

Increasingly, many adults are becoming "soccer parents" as a result of the rise in popularity of that sport in the United States, particularly among young children. A common feature of soccer games for very young players (e.g., four- and five-year-olds) is that no score is kept. Therefore, no one wins (or loses) the match. Interestingly, we have observed that even young players sometimes cannot accept such an outcome, despite their parents' explanation that "It's just a game; it's just for fun; it doesn't matter." The young players continue to ask, "Okay, but who *won?*"

Clearly, the soccer programs are structured to allow players to focus on skill development and to avoid the harmful effects of competition at an early age. Yet competition is a feature, for better or worse, of much of American culture. What is necessary, particularly in classrooms, is a healthy balance between removing all competition and overreliance on competitive motivation.

Previous research on the educational effects of competition suggests that it reduces rather than enhances student motivation and performance; instead of teaching students to strive for success, it can instead teach them to strive to avoid failure (see, e.g., Eschemann, 1992; Holt, 1982). Taken to the extreme, fear of failure can induce students to use unethical means (e.g., cheating or other unacceptable methods) to boost test performance and raise their odds of success. We recommend that testing and grading systems in which the focus is on comparing students to one another be used cautiously. For example, norm-referenced tests, grading on a curve, or the practice of having students exchange and grade one another's papers highlights the differences between students, encourages competition, and can induce heightened anxiety about evaluation.

Praise Construction

A strong recollection of one author of this book (GJC) from his pre-service teacher education courses, taken in the 1970s and 1980s, was the high place afforded to praise as a tool of effective teachers. As undergraduates, we learned that negative words should be banned from our vocabularies as future teachers. Classroom rules should be phrased not as "Don't hit another student" but as "Be kind to one another." Red pens for correcting papers were out; only positive comments should be written on papers. Likewise, we were instructed to avoid correcting students when they engaged in bad behavior but to praise them when they engaged in good behavior. Though the memories may have become less accurate over time, my distinct recollection is that universal, unequivocal praise was seen as the panacea for all classroom problems and that, to some extent, that principle has been slow to fade.

As it turns out, unqualified, unconditional praise actually can be harmful for students. It is a simple thing, yet the way in which a teacher or parent praises a child's performance can affect subsequent performances. For example, one recent study demonstrated that praising a student for his or her ability or intelligence had more negative consequences for that student's subsequent achievement motivation; praise for the student's effort had more positive consequences (Mueller & Dweck, 1998). The authors interpreted those findings to mean that students who were praised for their ability believed that test scores were a measure of their intelligence and so would continue to choose tasks that demonstrated their abilities. In contrast, students praised for their effort subsequently attempted tasks that offered greater learning opportunities. If a student perceives that tests are a reflection of ability, is praised for test performance, and subsequently experiences failure on a test, he or she is more likely to attribute the failure to (poor) ability than is a student who is praised for effort. As one author has noted, "This suggests that children may be more resilient to the effects of poor test performance if the 'intelligence' aspect of these is minimized" (McDonald, 2001, p. 31). To close the loop, as we have seen previously, students' self-perceptions of low ability are a significant contributor to test anxiety. Thus, cautious use of praise so that it focuses on and reinforces the effort that a student has expended is a strategy that teachers can use to help prevent a key precursor of test anxiety.

Assessment Literacy

People are often uncomfortable with unfamiliar things or with things they don't understand. In education—for whatever reason—many students, parents, teachers, and administrators do not understand the testing process, how tests are developed, what test scores mean, or how they can be used. An entire book might be written on that topic alone, but for now we will be content to note that in most states formal coursework in assessment is not required to obtain licensure as a teacher; even less assessment competence is required for an administrative credential. Having taught college-level courses in assessment and having many years of experience in elementary and secondary school classrooms, we can attest to what one testing expert has referred to as a general "apathy concerning testing and grading" (Hills, 1991) among educators.

There is an abundance of supporting literature that documents the generally low level of what Stiggins (1991, 1995) has called assessment literacy. Our own affections tempt us to use this opportunity to go on at length at this juncture, describing the fundamentals of assessment. However, our respect for the reader (and our desire to sustain your interest in this chapter!) compels us to resist the impulse to provide a primer on topics ranging from psychometrics to statistics. Instead, we will content ourselves with a summary of the state of affairs of assessment literacy in education, and with hypothesizing that one reason for what we perceive to be mistrust of or dislike for tests is rooted in a lack of pervasive grounding in how tests should be constructed, administered, scored, and used.

Actually, we are unable to resist the impulse completely. Over the years, we have noticed that large-scale student testing often is misunderstood. Each of the authors of this book has maintained a list of myths about testing that have made their way into the lingua franca of teaching. We recognize our tendency to confuse the reader's patience for enjoyment of a topic that is dear to us, so we will keep our treatment short and, we hope, relevant to the interests of most readers. Thus, rather than providing technical explanations to help dispel the myths, we have decided to simply create a table (Table 6–5) that lists the myths alongside the realities. (Of course, for any reader who is interested in more technical explanations or elaborations for the realities, we would happily oblige.)

Table 6–5   Thirteen Testing Myths Exposed

	Myth	Reality
1	"Someone at the state Department of Education writes the test questions."	False.
		In most states, test questions are written by teachers from within the state who are currently practicing in the grade and subject for which they are writing questions.
		In some states, it is difficult to get teacher volunteers to write questions. In those states, content specialists from an outside testing company may be hired to create first drafts of questions. In those cases, states require local teachers to review and approve the items before they can be used on a state test. Even before item writing begins, teacher panels are regularly involved in determining the objectives that will be covered by a test (i.e., the content standards) for each grade and subject. They are also regularly involved in reviewing and approving all open-ended items, essay prompts, scoring rubrics, etc.
2	"The questions on the test are biased."	Probably false.
		Test questions must survive at least two bias-screening stages before they are considered for use on a state-mandated test.
		First, committees of teachers representing various ethnic groups, and specialists in gender, age, and SES stereotyping review all items and reject those that are offensive, inappropriate, insensitive, or potentially biased. Second, items are tried out (called "field testing") with small samples of students and are statistically examined to determine if certain groups of students (e.g., females, African Americans, nonnative speakers of English) are disadvantaged by any item. If so, the item is rejected or revised.
		(As an aside, we note that research on testing indicates that the presence of bias in large-scale high-stakes tests typically is much less of a problem than the bias found in classroom assessments.)
3	"Students' essays and other open-ended item responses are scored by out-of-state, part-time, unemployed cosmetologists."	Possibly true, but . . .
		In most states, because testing typically occurs at the end of the school year, it is not possible to assemble enough qualified teachers willing to spend some of their summer vacation scoring open-ended items. As a result, many states rely on one of a few specialized companies in the United States that are capable of scoring large numbers of student essays, etc., in a relatively short time.
		The scoring companies screen and hire qualified personnel on a temporary basis to read and score student work. Qualifications depend on the subject area to be scored. For example, a college degree in English or related area would be required for a person to be considered for scoring

Myth	Reality
	student essays in language arts. Thus, in theory, a cosmetologist who held a degree in colonial literature could qualify. However, even qualified applicants must undergo extensive training and monitoring to ensure that the scores they assign are faithful to the approved scoring rubric.
	Again, because most state testing is done during a short time period at the end of the school year, the scoring companies do not need to retain scorers on a full-time basis throughout the year.
4 "I've noticed that there are different forms of a test mixed in for my classroom. One of the forms is harder than the other."	False. The test forms that a teacher distributes to a class may differ. The difference is not in the items that count toward students' scores (which are the same, so they are equally difficult), but in other items, embedded within the tests, that are only being tried out to see how they perform (see Myth 2). In order to try out many new items (because not all of them turn out to be good) several forms of a test usually are produced, each with a different set of field-test items included.
5 "The test makers are always changing the score required for passing (or to be classified as *proficient*, etc.)."	Partly true. Technically, the level of performance required to pass or be classified as *proficient*, etc., does not change from year to year. It is, however, nearly impossible to produce tests year after year that are of *exactly* the same level of difficulty. Suppose that a state test contained 50 items each year. Further suppose that a score of 35 correct answers was required to pass the test last year, and that this year's test is slightly more difficult. In this situation, it would be unfair to hold this year's students to a standard of 35 correct answers. Using statistical analysis, it is possible to detect small differences in the difficulty of, say, this year's test compared to last year's. Using a process called equating, small adjustments are made to the passing score for the current year (it may be 34 instead of 35), to account for the fact that the current test is slightly harder. It is important to recognize, however, that *the level of knowledge, skill, or ability required to meet the standard does not change.*
6 "The tests are designed to produce a bell-shaped curve distribution of scores."	Sometimes true, sometimes false. Norm-referenced tests (e.g., the *Iowa Tests of Basic Skills* or intelligence tests) often produce a bell-shaped (i.e., "normal") distribution of scores. They are designed in such a way as to result in a spread of scores.

(Continued)

Table 6–5 (Continued)

	Myth	Reality
		State-mandated standards-referenced or criterion-referenced tests are never designed to yield a normal score distribution. In fact, most everyone involved would probably prefer a result in which all scores were high.
7	"Only a certain percentage of students can pass the test."	False. This relates to Myth 6. In norm-referenced systems (e.g., grading on the curve) the statement may be true. However, state-mandated achievement tests for students are designed so that, if instruction is adequate and focused on the state content standards, and if all students learn and are motivated to do well, all students *could* pass (or be classified as *proficient*, etc.). Technically, if the opposite circumstances existed, all students could fail. In reality, instruction, effort, ability, motivation, etc., all vary, so pass/fail rates also vary.
8	"The test questions don't address the things I teach in my classroom."	Potentially a big problem. As indicated previously (see Myth 1), teachers are regularly involved in determining what knowledge and skills are to be covered by a state test (i.e., the state's content standards). If the questions on a test don't appear to match what is taught in a classroom, one of two serious problems may be present: (1) classroom instruction is focused on the content standards, but the test is not well-aligned to the standards; or (2) the test is well-aligned to the content standards, but the classroom instruction is not.
9	"Tests only measure test-taking skills or how well a student can guess."	Mostly false. While it is true that students with better test-taking skills are likely to do better on tests, that is not the same as saying that tests *only* measure those skills. On the contrary, when tests are designed and built to meet a set of content standards, they measure content-related achievement to a much greater degree than any other knowledge or skill. A student with no mastery of the state's math objectives is not likely to pass a state's math test, no matter how exceptional his or her test-taking skills are. As regards guessing, it may be surprising to learn that guessing is considered when the passing scores for tests are established. If, for example, a test consists of four-option multiple-choice items, the method used for setting the passing score will take into account the fact that a score of 25% correct could be obtained by sheer guessing. And guessing on tests is not just "noise." Informed guessing is a helpful real-world skill. Guessing can help distinguish students with greater knowledge or skill from those with lesser. For example, suppose Student A can eliminate two wrong answers and makes an informed guess from the remaining two choices. He or she likely has a better

Myth	Reality
	understanding of the content than Student B who must randomly guess from among all four choices. All things being equal over an entire test, Student A would—and probably should—receive a higher total score than Student B.
10 "Test scores are meaningless because they only reflect what a student did on a particular day."	Mostly false. Strictly speaking, a test score is a reflection of what a student did on a particular occasion. If, for example, a student was fatigued, "in the zone," upset, lucky, cheating, etc. when taking a test, then the student's score may be lower or higher than his or her true level of knowledge or skill. On the other hand, test results are routinely analyzed to determine their reliability. Reliability is an indication of how confident we can be that the same or similar scores would be obtained on a different occasion. Reliability co-efficients range from 0.0 to 1.0, with 1.0 indicating perfect reliability. High-stakes achievement tests typically have a reliability of .90 or greater. Thus, while they are not perfect (and any given student can still have a very good or a very bad day), we can routinely count on large-scale test data to yield consistent, dependable results.
11 "On the math test, a student in my class performed better on the number sense portion than on the geometry portion. I should work with the student on geometry."	Maybe. Maybe not. As noted in the response to Myth 10, total scores (e.g., a student's total math score) are highly reliable. This occurs because total scores in a subject area are usually based on a fairly large sample of items (e.g., 40 or more). The same cannot be said of the smaller components (sometimes called subtests or strands) that compose the total. Subareas often consist of considerably fewer items and, consequently, are not nearly as reliable. In addition, because subtests are not usually equally difficult, a lower score on a very hard subtest might actually reflect better performance than a higher score on an easier subtest. Most state testing programs should caution users that a student's subtest scores should not be used to make intervention decisions for that student. The soundest strategy would be to analyze average subtest performance for a group (say, a classroom, or all third graders in a district) and adjust instruction accordingly.
12 "Tests don't measure many of the most important outcomes of education, like creativity, honesty, ability to work with others, and so on."	True. In defense of large-scale tests, however, they don't claim to do this. These characteristics are not measured easily or well by tests. It is likely that the educational system will always rely on the professional judgment of educators to gauge how well these objectives are being accomplished.
13 "You can't judge from a student's test score how hard I work as a teacher or the quality of instruction in my classroom."	True. Student achievement tests aren't designed to do this either—only to gauge how much students have learned.

We recognize that a casual review of Table 6–5 will not do much to advance the cause of assessment literacy. However, we assert that there is a strong, inverse relationship between assessment literacy and test anxiety, so we want to promote greater understanding of testing whenever possible. In the case of test anxiety, we know that when students are faced with a test and are unsure where it comes from, how scores will be calculated, or what will be done with the scores, the unknown factors heighten test anxiety—as, for that matter, they do in a teacher who is charged with administering that test. The modest information provided in the table might help to alleviate some concerns and reduce some fears about the previously unknown.

Our general recommendations are twofold. First, teachers should obtain as much information as possible about a large-scale norm-referenced or state-mandated standards-referenced test. Though not as complete or user-friendly as we would prefer, most state department of education Web sites have an abundance of information and answers to common questions about testing and are designed with the needs of educators in mind. Similarly, publishers of major tests make such information available on their Web sites and in printed materials. We know (from experience) that it can sometimes be difficult to track down the answer to a specific question, but we also can affirm that the information is almost always there. As much of the information as possible should, as appropriate, be communicated in relevant ways to students and parents.

Second, for less-formal classroom tests, we urge teachers to provide students and parents with as much information about a test or graded assignment as possible. This recommendation is repeated from earlier in this chapter (see Table 6–3), but the strategy is effective for reducing test anxiety.

Review Scores, Tests, and Work

A test score is more than just a number or a means to a grade, and there is much more information about a student's knowledge, skill, or comprehension to be gleaned from test performance. Of particular value are the instructional insights that test results can provide for teachers. Test results can help teachers see what topics students are grasping and can highlight other areas that might warrant review, different instructional approaches, refinements of lesson plans, and so on. In well-functioning assessment systems, the process includes a feedback loop that informs instruction (see Cizek, 1995). Our experience with both large-scale tests and classroom assessments suggests that the instructional feedback loop functions more effectively for tests that teachers construct for classroom use than it does for their larger-scale counterparts. We recommend that teachers attempt to use information from both kinds of assessments to foster integrated instruction/ assessment systems focused on improvement. And we recommend that state testing agencies begin to devote more resources to the creation of materials and services that make large-scale test data more useful for instructional planning.

Students and parents, too, should learn more from a test than just a score. Reviewing students' work can help illuminate what the student knows, what he or she needs to work on, and any misunderstandings or misconceptions he or she may have. Effective review of test results encompasses more than just making sure a student can arrive at the correct answer. Parents can assist children by having them rework problems and explain their thinking aloud, taking time to listen to their logic and thought patterns, and noting gaps in their knowledge. Again, as was mentioned previously, perhaps the greatest strategy for alleviating test anxiety is to instill the feeling of mastery and confidence that can be gained from an in-depth review of test performance.

Summary

As we have seen in previous chapters, test anxiety is a complex and multifaceted issue. There is no single strategy that will cure it instantaneously or prevent its development. Because the circumstances that precede and surround it are so diverse, it must be addressed in a multimodal fashion that enlists the combined efforts of students, parents, teachers, and administrators.

Previous research has provided some techniques and strategies to reduce test anxiety, but there is also much work left to do. Most of the research on intervention has been conducted with and designed for students at the college and university level. As one researcher has noted, "There is a serious lack of research on test-anxiety reduction programs for primary, middle and secondary students" (Ergene, 2003, p. 325). However, some effective strategies for elementary and secondary students are known, and we have tried to gather them together in this chapter. We hope that the strategies described in this chapter are helpful not only to teachers but also, ultimately, to students for whom test anxiety interferes with learning and precludes the true demonstration of knowledge or skills on tests.

7

Conclusions
and Next Steps

In 1987, a published article on test anxiety noted that the phenomenon was then observing its 35th birthday (Hembree, 1988). If the time of birth was accurately pegged, that would mean test anxiety is in its mid-50s today, entering those golden years.

With the increase in intelligence testing, aptitude testing, and placement testing in schools witnessed in the 1950s, it is no surprise that interest in test anxiety was spawned at that time. Over the years, the scientific interest in test anxiety has grown. Hembree (1988) counts approximately 30 studies on test anxiety in the 1950s, 150 in the 1960s, and 271 in the 1970s. During the period from the 1950s to the 1970s, nearly all of the test-anxiety instruments now in use were developed. However, by the 1980s, the number of studies of test anxiety began to dwindle, and few new instruments were developed or theoretical perspectives advanced. By the 1990s, social scientists largely began to ignore test anxiety.

Today, interest in test anxiety is again being stimulated. Again, the field of education is witnessing a growth in the amount of testing. In general, intelligence testing no longer commands much respect or receives much use in U.S. schools. But every-pupil achievement testing in Grades 3 through 8 plus high school, nascent accountability systems, federal legislation such as the No Child Left Behind Act and the Individuals with Disabilities Education Act (IDEA), and mandates to monitor yearly student progress means that testing is perhaps more prominent, more pervasive, and more consequential for students and educators than at any other time. With the increasing frequency of and consequences associated with high-stakes tests, we also join in the call for greater attention to be paid to the problem of test anxiety.

However, we do not want to leave readers with the impression that real, debilitating test anxiety—in contrast to the normal sense of apprehension that nearly everyone experiences prior to an evaluative event—affects all students or even a majority of them. On the contrary, the preponderance of research and professional opinion suggests that the effects of test anxiety are limited and that, to some extent, the detrimental effect of test anxiety on some students is offset by its beneficial effect on others. As Ball (1995) has stated:

> If the impact of test anxiety is intense and widespread, then the research evidence has yet to show it. The possibility that test anxiety produces an intensely negative impact for a few students cannot be refuted; if it does, however, it probably produces a mildly positive impact for many students, resulting in little overall impact. (p. 113)

Obviously, the craft of teaching comprises a complex mix of factors, considerations, contexts, and decisions. If test anxiety is to be addressed, it must first be brought to our attention, and those involved in education, including parents and the students themselves, must be able to recognize test anxiety, to differentiate real test anxiety from normal nervousness about testing, to be alert to the factors that are often associated with test anxiety, and to provide appropriate interventions to help students whose real levels of knowledge and skill are masked by the presence of test anxiety. It has been our intention to provide information relevant to these goals in Chapters 1, 2, 3, 4, and 6, respectively. Professional educators (including teachers, counselors, and school psychologists) also may want to gauge levels of test anxiety among classrooms of students or for individual students at a given time, or they may wish to use the instruments we listed in Chapter 5 in a pre- and post-fashion, to evaluate the effectiveness of test-anxiety interventions.

Tables 7–1 and 7–2 present a summary of simple interventions that we think will be helpful to educators and parents who want a Cliffs Notes checklist of proven strategies for preventing and tempering the effects of test anxiety. In addition, Appendix B contains several resources for those who want additional information or a more

Table 7–1   Checklist of Intervention Strategies—Educators

_____   DO provide structured lessons with advance organizers and opportunities for review

_____   DO provide direct instruction and practice in metacognitive skills

_____   DO balance curriculum/content coverage with opportunities for reflection

_____   DO emphasize learning over grades or rewards

_____   DO communicate the importance and seriousness of testing

_____   DO promote an honest, open atmosphere regarding testing and grading

_____   DO listen to and consider students' comments about tests

_____   DO consider allowing students to work in groups of two or more for some tests

_____   DO understand and communicate to students the purposes and characteristics of the tests they take and the uses of the results

_____   DO use varied assessment techniques

_____   DO provide students with practice in tested skills and test formats

_____   DO give frequent, brief tests for (primarily) instructional purposes

_____   DO ensure that testing conditions are safe, comfortable, and distraction-free

_____   DO promote mastery of tested knowledge or skills

_____   DO teach appropriate test-taking skills

_____   DO encourage independence, self-confidence, and self-efficacy in students

_____   DO use praise to support student effort and achievement

_____   DO review student work for deeper understanding

_____   DON'T introduce additional pressure or anxiety into high-stakes testing situations

_____   DON'T communicate unrealistic or overly high expectations

_____   DON'T use "pop" quizzes

_____   DON'T use timed (speeded) tests unless speed of response or ability to work under pressure are the characteristics intended to be measured

_____   DON'T use grades punitively

_____   DON'T let test motivation or test preparation activities heighten test anxiety

_____   DON'T engage in or permit actions that threaten the validity of test scores (e.g., cheating, unethical test-preparation activities)

(Continued)

Table 7–1 (Continued)

_____ DON'T deviate from the guidelines for administering standardized tests

_____ DON'T overemphasize test results or consequences

_____ DON'T communicate negative expectations

_____ DON'T overemphasize competition in the classroom

Table 7–2   Checklist of Intervention Strategies—Parents

_____ DO emphasize learning over grades or rewards

_____ DO communicate the importance and seriousness of testing

_____ DO understand and communicate to students the purposes and characteristics of the tests they take and the uses of the results

_____ DO provide students with frequent review and practice in tested content

_____ DO encourage independence, self-confidence, and self-efficacy in children

_____ DO maintain open communications and positive family relationships

_____ DO use praise to support student effort and achievement

_____ DO review student work for deeper understanding

_____ DON'T introduce additional pressure or anxiety into high-stakes testing situations

_____ DON'T communicate unrealistic or overly high expectations

_____ DON'T use grades punitively

_____ DON'T permit actions that threaten the validity of test scores (e.g., cheating)

_____ DON'T overemphasize test results or consequences

_____ DON'T communicate negative expectations

in-depth treatment of many of the aspects of test anxiety that we have addressed in this book.

What does the future hold for test anxiety? It is uncertain whether scientific interest in the topic will once again be stimulated to the degree it was in the 1970s. However, we note that an educational trend seems to be that when the U.S. education system faces challenges—for example, placing a man on the moon, deepening knowledge in mathematics and science, imparting technological skills, or instituting systems of accountability—the way that the system responds to those challenges invariably affects students in both positive and negative ways. Test anxiety seems to ebb and flow as the responses of U.S. schools to educational challenges wax and wane.

In general, we are optimistic regarding both the capacity of U.S. schools to respond to challenges and the capability of social scientists to provide new insights into test anxiety. We have one concern about diverging trends, however, and we currently are unable to foresee how it will resolve itself.

That concern involves what might be called the fear of the unknown. In general, we think that two features of American education are here to stay. The first is accountability systems and high-stakes testing with important consequences for students and educators alike. If anything, we expect the trend toward greater accountability to increase.

The other concern relates to currently accepted professional practice in schools. In everyday classrooms, students rarely face any assessments for which there are consequences. As teachers ourselves, we regularly permitted students to do various additional work for extra credit at the end of a marking period; we permitted students to retake tests to obtain higher scores; we permitted tests and quizzes to be taken with essentially no time limits or to be completed as "take-home tests"; we often based grades on what a group of students achieved; and we incorporated factors such as effort, cooperation, class participation, and the like into final grades. Our experience (and the research evidence) suggests that such practices are ubiquitous in American schools. And although we believe that there still is a place for these practices and that individual teachers' professional judgments ought to determine whether or when such practices are appropriate, we also believe that it is possible that a steady diet of such practices may not have been in our students' best interests.

We hypothesize that exclusive reliance on such practices creates a fear of the unknown for many students. The end-of-spring, state-mandated test in mathematics may be the only time during a student's school year that he or she faces a test that actually has consequences. And all of the features of that test differ from what the student has become accustomed to in classroom assessments. This must surely make the event one that triggers great unease for many students.

In the future, we think that research might focus on understanding the educational practices that contribute to test anxiety and on developing a better understanding of how test anxiety is transmitted to students. In addition, we think that changing testing and making testing more relevant and informative to students, teachers, and parents will go a long way toward reducing the anxiety associated with testing.

In closing, it seems appropriate to us that a book on testing and anxiety should end with a test. Therefore, we ask readers to turn now to Appendix D and complete the 87-item test we have prepared, covering the contents of this book. There is a 20-minute time limit.

Just kidding.

Appendix A:
Glossary

Ability test   a kind of test, the purpose of which is to measure potential for achievement. Sometimes also referred to as *aptitude tests*. Nearly all ability tests used in classrooms are of the standardized, commercially produced variety, such as the *Otis-Lennon School Abilities Test* and the *Cognitive Abilities Test,* which can be used in conjunction with an achievement test to derive ability/achievement comparisons that describe the extent to which a student is under- or overachieving in school, given his or her measured potential. Another common use of ability tests such as the *Wechsler Intelligence Scale for Children–Revised* (WISC-R) is to identify students for placement in certain programs (e.g., special education or gifted education).

Achievement test   a kind of test, the purpose of which is to measure a student's attainment of knowledge or skill. Achievement tests can be developed for either informal, classroom use (e.g., spelling tests, chemistry lab reports, oral questioning in class) or for formal, large-scale use (e.g., state-mandated achievement tests, the *Iowa Tests of Basic Skills,* the *Terra Nova,* and others).

Anxiety   internal feelings of dread or tension that a person experiences (either in a specific situation or as an enduring characteristic) in the absence of a real, tangible threat to the person. Anxiety is an unrealistic or exaggerated response to the perceived threat.

Assessment   the process of gathering and synthesizing multiple sources of information for the purpose of describing or making decisions about a student. The term *assessment* has been borrowed from fields such as medicine and counseling, in which a patient or client may be given a variety of tests, the results of which must be synthesized—that is, analyzed and interpreted—by a single professional or a team of experts. In education, assessment pertains most accurately to contexts such as special education, in which an individualized education program (IEP) is planned for a student based on a variety of sources of information about the student. (Note: The term *assessment* is—incorrectly, though increasingly—used simply as a synonym for a test or assignment.)

Battery   a collection of tests. For example, the *Iowa Tests of Basic Skills* (ITBS) is one of several large-scale testing programs that offer what is called a complete battery. This version of the ITBS actually is several fairly short individual tests (or "subtests") covering discrete areas such as reading, language arts, mathematics, study skills, and so on. This version of the ITBS is not really a single test but is more accurately referred to as a battery of tests.

Construct validity   characteristics measured by many tests, referred to as constructs because they usually are not directly observable but instead are "constructed." Constructs are, as one researcher has described them, "the products of informed scientific imagination" (Crocker & Algina, 1986, p. 4). Gathering construct validity evidence for a test involves demonstrating that the instrument is well aligned with theories about the construct the instrument claims to measure and demonstrating that the scores on the instrument truly reflect varying degrees of the characteristic.

Constructed-response   an item format in which the test taker must create a response. Examples of constructed-response formats include essays, short-answer items, speeches, projects, and so forth.

Content standards   statements that describe the specific knowledge, skills, or abilities in a subject area that students are expected to acquire by a given age or grade level.

Convergent validity   one of several possible types of validity evidence. Convergent validity evidence is obtained by examining the relationship (usually the correlation) between scores on two tests designed to measure the same or similar characteristics. For example, if a scientist developed a new measure of intelligence, one way to gather validity evidence would be to demonstrate that scores on the new instrument were strongly related to scores for the same sample of test takers on an existing, accepted intelligence test.

Correlation   a statistical process used to estimate the strength of the linear relationship that may exist between two variables. The term is also used to refer to the actual number, ranging from −1.0 to 1.0, that results from calculations to obtain the estimate. In simplest terms, correlation can be understood by breaking the word itself into parts: *co* and *relation;* it is the extent to which scores on two things are related to each other.

Criterion-referenced test (CRT)   a kind of test, the purpose of which is to gauge whether a student knows or can do specific things. CRTs may be developed and used in informal ways for classroom use, or may be instituted on a larger scale. In either case, the content of the test would be highly specific, the test would be tightly linked to specific objectives, and a criterion for judging success on the test would be specified a priori. Some examples of CRTs would include weekly spelling tests, driver's license tests, vocational performance tests, and so on, with the key characteristic of such tests being the presence of the specific criteria.

The simplest illustration of a CRT is the road portion of a driver's license test. In the parallel parking portion, the candidate for a license must meet certain criteria: for example, parking the car within a marked area, in 4 minutes or less, without knocking over more than one orange pylon. A person's success or failure—manifested in whether or not the person gets a driver's license—does not depend on how well other candidates perform. In theory, all drivers could pass or all could fail. There is no distinction between one candidate who parks the vehicle perfectly in the middle of the space, in only 2 minutes, with no pylons knocked over, and the candidate who parks awkwardly within the space, in just under 4 minutes, and knocks one pylon over. Both candidates met the criteria.

Effect size   the difference, expressed in standard deviation units, between two treatments or conditions. For example, suppose that a researcher conducted a study on whether students who attended a certain test preparation program obtained higher SAT scores than a comparable group of students who did not receive the test coaching. The researcher would calculate the mean SAT performance of both groups; say, 600 for the students who received the training and 550 for those who did not. The researcher would then divide the difference by the standard deviation of the SAT scores—for example, by 100—to determine the effect size (ES). In this hypothetical example, the effect size would be $50/100 = .50$. The ES of .50 would mean that, on average, the group that received the test preparation performed about one-half of a standard deviation better than the group that received no coaching—a fairly large effect.

Emotionality   theoretically, the physiological reactions to stress, including the stress associated with testing. Such reactions include changes in heart rate, respiration, and so on.

Error   any factor that causes a student's test score to be higher or lower than the student's "true" level of knowledge, skill, or ability. According to psychometric theories, the score that a student is assigned on a test (called an observed score) is a fallible representation of what the student truly knows or can do. Observed scores are only indirect and imperfect representations of the student's underlying true level of knowledge or skill. We cannot ever know with certainty the true level of knowledge or skill, so we must make do with imperfect estimates. Observed test scores are imperfect because they are the result not only of the student's knowledge or skill but also of other factors, such as the testing conditions, the student's mood at the time of testing, the clarity of the printed questions or tasks, the student's good (or bad) luck at guessing when he or she does not know the answer, any of which could result in a student's observed score being higher or lower than the student's true performance would be. All of these other factors are lumped under the general heading of error.

Evaluation   the process of ascribing value or worth to a test score or performance. For example, a student may earn 40 out of 50 points on a term paper. Evaluation takes place when a judgment of value or worth accompanies the score. The most common form of ascribing value can be seen in the assigning of grades. In this case, awarding a B to a student who scored 40 out of 50 would be evaluation.

Fear   internal feelings of dread or tension that a person experiences (either in a specific situation or as an enduring characteristic) in the presence of a real, tangible threat to the person. Fear is an appropriate or realistic response to the threat.

Field testing   the process of administering test items or tasks to test takers under circumstances in which the test takers' performances are not of primary concern. Typically, students' scores on a field test do not "count." Rather, the items or tasks are administered so that test makers can judge how well the items or tasks themselves perform. Eventually, items that survive an initial tryout in field testing and that are judged to be of sufficiently high quality become eligible to be used on a subsequent test that *does* count for the test takers.

High-stakes   a term (along with its opposite, *low-stakes*) referring to the severity of the consequences associated with performance on a test or assignment. For example, if a test is used to determine whether a high school student can graduate, the consequences of passing or failing it are obviously serious, and the test would be called high-stakes. On the other hand, weekly observations made by an elementary school teacher regarding her students' participation in class may be verbally communicated to parents during a parent-teacher conference, or may even count toward a student's "effort" grade, but serious consequences or decisions about a student would not ordinarily follow. Such an evaluation would be termed low-stakes.

Inference   an interpretation, conclusion, or meaning drawn about some underlying, usually unobservable characteristic, based on an observed sample of information, behavior, actions, or responses.

Item   a question on a test or assignment. If the question was written using a selected-response format, the item would ordinarily consist of what is called a stem (the part that introduces the question) and what are called options (often labeled A, B, C, D, or similarly). If the question was developed using a constructed-response format, the item would usually consist of a prompt (the written or other material introducing the task) and a related rubric (the scoring guide used to rate the performance or the responses to the task).

Metacognition   the mental activity of thinking about one's own thinking processes and ideas. For example, suppose a student is working a mathematics problem. Along the way, the student silently wonders, "Did I follow each of the three steps that the teacher showed us?" or thinks, "I've made the same mistake on the last two problems; I wonder why I always forget to express my answer in lowest terms." The student's ruminations (i.e., cognitions) about his or her own thinking processes are referred to as metacognitive thoughts. Effective instruction usually includes explicit development of such metacognitive skills.

Norm-referenced test (NRT)   a kind of test, the purpose of which is to describe the relative standing of students at a particular grade level. NRTs provide information about how a student's performance compares with a reference group of students, called the norm group. Familiar examples of NRTs include the *Iowa Tests of Basic Skills* (ITBS), the *TerraNova*, the SAT, the *Wechsler Intelligence Scale for Children–Revised* (WISC-R), and the *Graduate Record Examinations* (GRE).

Norms   test results and other characteristics of test takers, usually drawn from a representative sample of some population. Subsequently, test results for those who take a test at a later date can be compared to the data from the norm group to determine the relationship of the test taker to that group.

Overlearning   the acquisition of knowledge or skill to a level beyond a specified degree of mastery. Overlearning usually requires repetition and practice to the point that the knowledge or skill can be demonstrated in an almost automatic way.

Percentile Rank (PR)   a norm-referenced score that indicates the percentage of a norm group that a test taker's score exceeds. For example, a PR of 75 would indicate that a test taker's score was higher than 75% of the scores in the norm group.

Psychometrics   a branch of psychology that studies the development, administration, and scoring of tests, and the quality and meaning of test scores.

Reliability   the dependability of test scores. Because an assignment or test consists only of a sample of questions or tasks, and because both the students who respond and those who score the responses are susceptible to various unpredictabilities in their performance (called random errors), no score can be considered a perfectly dependable snapshot of a student's performance. Various methods can be used to quantify the degree of confidence that can be placed in students' scores. All of the methods result in a number called a reliability coefficient, which can take on any value from 0.0 to 1.0. A reliability coefficient of 0.0 would mean that the scores are completely undependable—no more useful for making decisions about students than flipping a coin or guessing. A reliability coefficient of 1.0 would indicate perfect dependability (the complete absence of random errors) and the potential for the test scores to be used with great confidence in decision making. Values between 0.0 and 1.0 indicate relative less (nearer to 0.0) or greater (nearer to 1.0) dependability.

Selected-response   an item format in which the test taker must choose the correct answer from alternatives provided. Examples of selected-response formats include multiple-choice, matching, and true/false formats.

Standardized   any uniform system of gathering information that is developed, administered, and scored under controlled conditions. Note, however, that the term *standardized* is unrelated to item format. Although the multiple-choice format comes to mind when thinking of a standardized test, such tests can be developed using any format.

The term also is sometimes used to refer to a test for which norms are available.

Standards-referenced test (SRT)   a kind of test, the purpose of which is to gauge a student's standing with respect to a set of content standards. Standards-referenced tests are similar to CRTs in that both attempt to describe the knowledge, skill, or abilities that students possess. Whereas CRTs express standards in terms of quantity and category (e.g., a percentage correct and passing/failing), SRTs link students' scores to concrete statements about what performance at the various levels means. State-mandated student testing for students in Grades K–12 in areas such as English language arts, mathematics, and so on typically would be considered to be SRTs, to the extent that the tests are aligned with the state's content standards in those subjects.

State   a temporary phenomenon or reaction that is evoked only in specific situations.

Test   any systematic sampling of a student's knowledge, skill, or ability. Ideally, those interested in a student's achievement would like to gather as much information as possible about what the student can do. Because of time, cost, or other considerations, they usually must settle instead for a sample of information or a limited amount of evidence. In order to gather as much information as is practical, tests are usually constructed to contain many different questions, tasks, essays, and so on, or some combination of these.

Test anxiety   a specific form of anxiety, comprising a combination of cognitive and physiological responses (worry and emotionality), and aroused in testing situations or similar situations involving personal evaluation.

Trait   an enduring characteristic of a person. A trait is a fairly stable characteristic that has pervasive effects or is evident in diverse aspects of a person's life.

Validity   the degree to which the conclusions yielded by any sample of behavior (e.g., a test, assignment, quiz, term paper, observation, or interview) are meaningful, accurate, and useful. Validity is the degree to which a student's performance results in decisions about the student or in inferences about the student's knowledge, skill, or ability that are "correct."

Worry   theoretically, the cognitive component of test anxiety, characterized by concerns about the likelihood and (negative) consequences of evaluation and failure.

Appendix B:
General Resources

There are numerous resources available for readers who are interested in further reading and information on test anxiety. The following annotated list is heterogenous. It includes books, Web sites, blogs, and other electronic sources, along with brief descriptions of each resource.

1. *Success with Test-Taking* **(Moke & Shermis, 2001)**
This book, audiotape, and companion manual is part of the Parents and Children Together series, which consists of read-along stories for children and practical guidelines for parents. This resource is designed for parents and teachers who want to learn specific strategies to help students become better test takers.
This resource may be purchased from

Family Learning Association
3925 Hagan St., Suite 101
Bloomington, IN 47401
Telephone: (800) 759-4723

Additional information about the Family Literacy Association and about other helpful resources offered by the Association is available at the organization's Web site:

http://reading.indiana.edu/www/famres/ptalk/pdf/011basic.pdf

2. **The *Number 2 Pencil***
The *Number 2 Pencil* takes its name from the writing instrument that is forever associated with standardized testing. The *Pencil* is a

blog—which is a contraction of the words *Web* and *log*. A blog is a contemporary, ongoing, interactive Web site that lists news and commentary by its host, and that invites reactions from readers whose responses and commentary are also posted and archived on the site.

The topics covered on the *Pencil* include test anxiety but are not limited to that topic. Test bias, test accommodations, college admissions testing, and all other topics related to testing are addressed. In addition to daily news related to testing, the blog also contains links to national testing organizations involved in K–12 and postsecondary testing, research associations, and an interesting link to "what a psychometrician looks like."

The host of the blog, Kimberly Swygert, is herself a psychometrician and is internationally respected for her work in computer-based testing and other psychometric subspecialties. The link to the *Number 2 Pencil* is

www.kimberlyswygert.com

3. The Buros Institute for Mental Measurement

The Buros Institute is located in Lincoln, at the University of Nebraska. It is the foremost clearinghouse for information about tests. The Institute publishes the *Mental Measurements Yearbook (MMY)*, which contains critical, independent reviews of published tests. The Institute also publishes *Tests in Print*, now in its sixth edition, which is a comprehensive bibliography of all known commercially available tests currently in print in the English language. Though it does not contain reviews of tests, as are found in *MMY, Tests in Print* does provide basic information about each test, including purpose, publisher, publication date, price, intended test population, and administration time. If an independent review for a test is available, the reference to *MMY* is also provided.

Finally, the Buros Institute Web site allows users to find tests, to locate and purchase test reviews online, and provides links to other Institute services. The main link to the Institute site is

http://www.unl.edu/buros/

The test search feature can be accessed directly from

http://buros.unl.edu/buros/jsp/search.jsp

4. The ETS Test Collection

Sponsored by the Educational Testing Service (ETS), the largest testing company in the world and developer of the familiar SAT college entrance examination, the test collection claims to be the largest in the world. It comprises information on over 20,000 tests developed by U.S. and foreign publishers as well as by individual scientists. The collection includes tests dating from the early 1900s to the present. In addition to descriptive information about tests for virtually any purpose, the site provides information on how copies of individual tests may be purchased. The link to the ETS Test Collection is

www.ets.org/testcoll

5. The Society for Test Anxiety Research

The Society for Test Anxiety Research (STAR) was founded in 1980 for the purpose of focusing scientific attention on and advancing knowledge related to test anxiety. In 1991, to reflect the broader interests of the organization, the name of the group was changed to the Stress and Anxiety Research Society, although the group retained the same acronym.

STAR is the single-largest academic association devoted to the study of test anxiety as well as general anxiety, stress, and coping. It is an international organization, with members from more than 35 countries. STAR sponsors an annual meeting at which, according to the STAR Web site, "members exchange research findings and clinical applications on a wide range of stress and anxiety related phenomena."

In addition to its annual meeting, STAR produces the journal *Anxiety, Stress, and Coping: An International Journal,* which serves as an outlet for worldwide dissemination of research on topics related to anxiety.

Information about *Anxiety, Stress, and Coping* can be obtained from one of the journal's coeditors:

Professor Krys Kaniasty
Department of Psychology
Indiana University of Pennsylvania
Indiana, PA 15705
Telephone: (724) 357–5559

The link to the STAR Web site is

http://www.star-society.org

6. Other Academic Books

Two scholarly book series on test anxiety are currently available in most college or university libraries. The first series, Advances in Test Anxiety Research, is published in Amsterdam by Swets and Zeitlinger Publishers for the Society for Test Anxiety Research (see Resource 5) and consists largely of the proceedings of the STAR annual conferences.

The second series, currently called Stress and Emotion: Anxiety, Anger, and Curiosity, has a long history of publication. Volumes 1 to 13 in the series (called Stress and Anxiety) span the years 1973 to 1991. The name of the series was changed in 1991, for volumes 14 to 16. The series contains much of the original work on test anxiety and on many related topics.

7. *Standards for Educational and Psychological Testing* (AERA/APA/NCME, 1999)

These standards represent the definitive professional guidelines for test development, administration, and use. The sponsors of the *Standards* are three prominent professional organizations committed to high-quality tests and high standards of test use. They include the American Educational Research Association, the American Psychological Association, and the National Council on Measurement in Education. *The Standards for Educational and Psychological Testing* is a book-length volume that addresses testing in all contexts, and primarily tests that are large-scale or have high stakes. Copies of the *Standards* can be located in all college or university libraries; it also may be purchased by contacting any of the sponsoring organizations.

8. *Rights and Responsibilities of Test Takers* (Joint Committee on Testing Practices, 2000)

This document represents the collaborative effort of numerous professional associations with an interest in advancing the quality and use of tests in the public interest. Collectively, the organizations have formed an entity called the Joint Committee on Testing Practices. Members of the Joint Committee include the National Council on Measurement in Education (NCME), the American Educational Research Association (AERA), the American Psychological Association (APA), the American Speech-Language-Hearing Association (ASHA), the National Association of School Psychologists (NASP), the National Association of Test Directors (NATD), and the American Counseling Association (ACA).

According to the preamble to *Rights and Responsibilities of Test Takers*, it is intended to enumerate and clarify the expectations that test takers may reasonably have about the testing process, and the expectations that those who develop, administer, and use tests may have of test takers. The knowledge of these expectations—and the commitment of the sponsoring organizations to follow and promote them—can have a positive effect on anxieties about testing. The complete document can be found at

http://www.apa.org/science/ttrr.html

9. *Code of Fair Testing Practices in Education* **(Joint Committee on Testing Practices, 2004)**

The Code represents another effort of the Joint Committee on Testing Practices to advance the quality and proper use of tests in the public interest. The Code details professional norms for sound testing practice, and it may be reproduced and disseminated freely. The Code promotes fairness and openness in testing; to the extent to which the guidelines in the Code are followed, anxiety about testing will be reduced for all concerned. Excerpts from the Code appear below.

The Code is available free of charge at

www.apa.org/science/fairtestcode.html

or by mail from:

Joint Committee on Testing Practices
Science Directorate, American Psychological Association
750 First Street, NE
Washington, DC 20002–4242

Excerpts from the Code of
Fair Testing Practices in Education

The *Code of Fair Testing Practices in Education* (the Code) is a guide for professionals in fulfilling their obligation to provide and use tests that are fair to all test takers regardless of age, gender, disability, race, ethnicity, national origin, religion, sexual orientation, linguistic background, or other personal characteristics. Fairness is a primary consideration in all aspects of testing. Careful standardization of tests and administration conditions helps to ensure that all test takers are given a comparable opportunity to demonstrate what they know and how they can perform in the area being tested.

Fairness implies that every test taker has the opportunity to prepare for the test and is informed about the general nature and content of the test, as appropriate to the purpose of the test. Fairness also extends to the accurate reporting of individual and group test results. Fairness is not an isolated concept, but must be considered in all aspects of the testing process.

The Code applies broadly to testing in education (admissions, educational assessment, educational diagnosis, and student placement), regardless of the mode of presentation, so it is relevant to conventional paper-and-pencil tests, to computer-based tests, and to performance tests. It is not designed to cover employment testing, licensure, or certification testing, or other types of testing outside the field of education. The Code is directed primarily at professionally developed tests used in formally administered testing programs. Although the Code is not intended to cover tests made by teachers for use in their own classrooms, teachers are encouraged to use the guidelines to help improve their testing practices.

The Code provides separate guidance for test developers and test users in four critical areas:

A. Developing and selecting appropriate tests

B. Administering and scoring tests

C. Reporting and interpreting test results

D. Informing test takers

A. Developing and Selecting Appropriate Tests

Test developers should provide the information and supporting evidence that test users need to select appropriate tests. Test users should select tests that meet the intended purpose and that are appropriate for the intended test takers.

Test Developers Should:

A-1. Provide evidence of what the test measures, the recommended uses, the intended test takers, and the strengths and limitations of the test, including the level of precision of the test scores.

A-2. Describe how the content and skills to be tested were selected and how the tests were developed.

A-3. Communicate information about a test's characteristics at a level of detail appropriate to the intended test users.

A-4. Provide guidance on the levels of skills, knowledge, and training necessary for appropriate review, selection, and administration of tests.

A-5. Provide evidence that the technical quality, including reliability and validity, of the test meets its intended purposes.

A-6. Provide to qualified test users representative samples of test questions or practice tests, directions, answer sheets, manuals, and score reports.

A-7. Avoid potentially offensive content or language when developing test questions and related materials.

A-8. Make appropriately modified forms of tests or administration procedures available for test takers with disabilities who need special accommodations.

A-9. Obtain and provide evidence on the performance of test takers of diverse subgroups, making significant efforts to obtain sample sizes that are adequate for subgroup analyses. Evaluate the evidence to ensure that differences in performance are related to the skills being assessed.

Test Users Should:

A-1. Define the purpose for testing, the content and skills to be tested, and the intended test takers. Select and use the most appropriate test based on a thorough review of available information.

A-2. Review and select tests based on the appropriateness of test content, skills tested, and content coverage for the intended purpose of testing.

A-3. Review materials provided by test developers and select tests for which clear, accurate, and complete information is provided.

A-4. Select tests through a process that includes persons with appropriate knowledge, skills, and training.

A-5. Evaluate evidence of the technical quality of the test provided by the test developer and any independent reviewers.

A-6. Evaluate representative samples of test questions or practice tests, directions, answer sheets, manuals, and score reports before selecting a test.

A-7. Evaluate procedures and materials used by test developers, as well as the resulting test, to ensure that potentially offensive content or language is avoided.

A-8. Select tests with appropriately modified forms or administration procedures for test takers with disabilities who need special accommodations.

A-9. Evaluate the available evidence on the performance of test takers of diverse subgroups. Determine to the extent feasible which performance differences may have been caused by factors unrelated to the skills being assessed.

B. Administering and Scoring Tests

Test developers should explain how to administer and score tests correctly and fairly. Test users should administer and score tests correctly and fairly.

Test Developers Should:

B-1. Provide clear descriptions of detailed procedures for administering tests in a standardized manner.

B-2. Provide guidelines on reasonable procedures for assessing persons with disabilities who need special accommodations or those with diverse linguistic backgrounds.

B-3. Provide information to test takers or test users on test question formats and procedures for answering test questions, including information on the use of any needed materials and equipment.

B-4. Establish and implement procedures to ensure the security of testing materials during all phases of test development, administration, scoring, and reporting.

B-5. Provide procedures, materials, and guidelines for scoring the tests, and for monitoring the accuracy of the scoring process. If scoring the test is the responsibility of the test developer, provide adequate training for scorers.

B-6. Correct errors that affect the interpretation of the scores and communicate the corrected results promptly.

B-7. Develop and implement procedures for ensuring the confidentiality of scores.

Test Users Should:

B-1. Follow established procedures for administering tests in a standardized manner.

B-2. Provide and document appropriate procedures for test takers with disabilities who need special accommodations or those with diverse linguistic backgrounds. Some accommodations may be required by law or regulation.

B-3. Provide test takers with an opportunity to become familiar with test question formats and any materials or equipment that may be used during testing.

B-4. Protect the security of test materials, including respecting copyrights and eliminating opportunities for test takers to obtain scores by fraudulent means.

B-5. If test scoring is the responsibility of the test user, provide adequate training to scorers and ensure and monitor the accuracy of the scoring process.

B-6. Correct errors that affect the interpretation of the scores and communicate the corrected results promptly.

B-7. Develop and implement procedures for ensuring the confidentiality of scores.

C. Reporting and Interpreting Test Results

Test developers should report test results accurately and provide information to help test users interpret test results correctly. Test users should report and interpret test results accurately and clearly.

Test Developers Should:

C-1. Provide information to support recommended interpretations of the results, including the nature of the content, norms or comparison groups, and other technical evidence. Advise test users of the benefits and limitations of test results and their interpretation. Warn against assigning greater precision than is warranted.

C-2. Provide guidance regarding the interpretations of results for tests administered with modifications. Inform test users of potential problems in interpreting test results when tests or test administration procedures are modified.

C-3. Specify appropriate uses of test results and warn test users of potential misuses.

C-4. When test developers set standards, provide the rationale, procedures, and evidence for setting performance standards or passing scores. Avoid using stigmatizing labels.

C-5. Encourage test users to base decisions about test takers on multiple sources of appropriate information, not on a single test score.

C-6. Provide information to enable test users to accurately interpret and report test results for groups of test takers, including information about who were and who were not [*sic*] included in the different groups being compared, and information about factors that might influence the interpretation of results.

C-7. Provide test results in a timely fashion and in a manner that is understood by the test taker.

C-8. Provide guidance to test users about how to monitor the extent to which the test is fulfilling its intended purposes.

Test Users Should:

C-1. Interpret the meaning of the test results, taking into account the nature of the content, norms or comparison groups, other technical evidence, and benefits and limitations of test results.

C-2. Interpret test results from modified test or test administration procedures in view of the impact those modifications may have had on test results.

C-3. Avoid using tests for purposes other than those recommended by the test developer unless there is evidence to support the intended use or interpretation.

C-4. Review the procedures for setting performance standards or passing scores. Avoid using stigmatizing labels.

C-5. Avoid using a single test score as the sole determinant of decisions about test takers. Interpret test scores in conjunction with other information about individuals.

C-6. State the intended interpretation and use of test results for groups of test takers. Avoid grouping test results for purposes not specifically recommended by the test developer unless evidence is obtained to support the intended use. Report procedures that were followed in determining who were and who were not [*sic*] included in the groups being compared and describe factors that might influence the interpretation of results.

C-7. Communicate test results in a timely fashion and in a manner that is understood by the test taker.

C-8. Develop and implement procedures for monitoring test use, including consistency with the intended purposes of the test.

D. Informing Test Takers

Under some circumstances, test developers have direct communication with the test takers and/or control of the tests, testing process, and test results. In other circumstances the test users have these responsibilities.

Test developers or test users should inform test takers about the nature of the test, test-taker rights and responsibilities, the appropriate use of scores, and procedures for resolving challenges to scores.

Test Developers and Test Users Should:

D-1. Inform test takers in advance of the test administration about the coverage of the test, the types of question formats, the directions, and appropriate test-taking strategies. Make such information available to all test takers.

D-2. When a test is optional, provide test takers or their parents/guardians with information to help them judge whether a test should be taken—including indications of any consequences that may result from not taking the test (e.g., not being eligible to compete for a particular scholarship)—and whether there is an available alternative to the test.

D-3. Provide test takers or their parents/guardians with information about rights test takers may have—to obtain copies of tests and completed answer sheets, to retake tests, to have tests rescored, or to have scores declared invalid.

D-4. Provide test takers or their parents/guardians with information about responsibilities test takers have, such as being aware of the intended purpose and uses of the test, performing at capacity, following directions, and not disclosing test items or interfering with other test takers.

D-5. Inform test takers or their parents/guardians how long scores will be kept on file and indicate to whom, under what circumstances, and in what manner test scores and related information will or will not be released. Protect test scores from unauthorized release and access.

D-6. Describe procedures for investigating and resolving circumstances that might result in canceling or withholding scores, such as failure to adhere to specified testing procedures.

D-7. Describe procedures that test takers, parents/guardians, and other interested parties may use to obtain more information about the test, to register complaints, and to have problems resolved.

Appendix C: Resources for Measuring Test Anxiety

This appendix provides greater detail about the technical qualities of the test-anxiety instruments mentioned in Chapter 5. Also included is a description of the peer-review process, which helps serve as a screen against poor-quality tests becoming widely used and is a mechanism for helping potential users evaluate the relative quality of tests that they are considering.

Quality Control in Testing

Perhaps regrettably, there is no governmental organization like the Food and Drug Administration to ensure that scientific evidence supports the claims of test publishers in the same way that the government demands evidence to support the claims made by makers of health foods, drugs, or vitamins. Fortunately, professionals in the area of educational and psychological measurement have taken it upon themselves to serve as quality-control specialists regarding the claims of those who produce tests. A key force behind this effort is the Buros Institute of Mental Measurements, located at the University of Nebraska (see Appendix B for contact information).

The Buros Institute publishes an important reference series related to testing, called the *Mental Measurements Yearbooks (MMY)*. Each volume of *MMY*—a new one is published every two to three years—contains a gold mine of information about hundreds of tests in a format that is very user friendly yet highly technically accurate and candid. It is not likely that the *MMY* series will be found in a local public library; however, it is almost certain that any college or university library will have the entire series in its reference section.

Perhaps the most distinguishing and important feature of *MMY* is that the series contains informative, concise, independent reviews of tests. The tests reviewed include achievement tests, aptitude tests, personality tests, psychological tests, career interest inventories, employment and professional tests—virtually any test likely to be encountered in an American school or workplace.

Here's how the independent review process works. To begin the process, any individual or group that produces a test can submit two complete sets of materials related to the test to Buros Institute. In addition to submitting actual copies of the instrument itself, the publisher or developer would ordinarily also submit copies of any test administration manual or directions, answer booklets or forms, answer keys, interpretive guides, and any technical documentation describing the research that bears on the technical quality of the instrument. First important note: If a test has not been reviewed in *MMY*, and if it has a publication date that is at least two to three years old, beware! Though not always the case, if an instrument has not been submitted for possible review and inclusion in *MMY*, it is a potential sign that the instrument may be of very poor or unknown quality. If a test developer or publisher knows that the instrument is of poor quality, they may not *want* it to be reviewed.

Once received by the staff at the Buros Institute, the compilation of materials related to an instrument is assigned to two independent reviewers. The reviewers are selected for their expertise in the area addressed by the test, for their knowledge of appropriate psychometrics, and for their independence and objectivity with respect to the authors or publishers of the instrument. In most cases, the independent reviewers hold Ph.D.s in the area covered by the test and most often are faculty members at major universities.

Independently, each reviewer then conducts an in-depth evaluation of all of the materials, including a review and appraisal of all technical documentation and research evidence supplied. A reviewer might administer the test him- or herself in order to assess the ease of administration and the directions for scoring the instrument. After each reviewer has become thoroughly familiar with the instrument, he or she prepares a brief summary of all aspects of the instrument: purpose, format, administration, scoring, reliability, validity, norms, and related characteristics as appropriate. The summaries of each reviewer are then checked and prepared for inclusion in a future volume of *MMY*.

When a potential user of a test wants information about the quality of the instrument, all he or she needs to do is locate the entries for the instrument in a volume of *MMY*. The user will find two independent, brief (usually 2–3 pages) reviews comprising concise information, description, and candid evaluation of the quality of the test. A potential user can also locate in *MMY* other instruments intended to measure the same characteristic and, by comparing the reviews for each of the instruments, decide which of the alternatives is of highest quality and which would be most appropriate for the intended application. We expect that readers of this book who have occasion to select or compare available tests–for any purpose, not limited to measurement of test anxiety—will find the *MMY* resource to be very valuable. (Additional information about this resource is also found in Appendix B.) We now turn to our own description and fairly detailed reviews of four test-anxiety instruments.

The *Suinn Test Anxiety Behavior Scale* (STABS)

The STABS is a 50-item scale designed to measure test anxiety in college freshman through seniors based on the normative data available. However, a review of the instrument itself suggests that it also may be appropriate for measuring relative test anxiety in high school students (although the norms tables provided would not be as accurate).

The instrument consists of brief statements related to testing, to which respondents choose one of five options. According to the directions for test, respondents are instructed to place a check mark in the box "that describes how much you are frightened" (Suinn, 1971a, p. 1) by the activity described in the statement. The five option choices are: *not at all, a little, a fair amount, much,* and *very much.* The complete directions and five sample activity statements are reproduced in Figure C–1.

The STABS can be administered to students individually or in groups and should take less than 20 minutes for nearly all students to complete. Scoring is accomplished by simply summing responses, with each *not at all* response counting as 1, *a little* counting as 2, and

Figure C–1   Sample Items from the *Suinn Test Anxiety Behavior Scale*

Directions: The items in the questionnaire refer to experiences that may cause fear or apprehension. For each item, place a check in the box under the column that describes how much you are frightened by it nowadays. Work quickly but be sure to consider each item individually.

	Not at all	A little	A fair amount	much	Very much
4. Turning my completed test paper in.	☐	☐	☐	☐	☐
5. Hearing the announcement of a coming test.	☐	☐	☐	☐	☐
13. Waiting for a test to be handed out.	☐	☐	☐	☐	☐
24. Looking at the clock to see how much time remains during an exam.	☐	☐	☐	☐	☐
25. Seeing the number of questions that need to be answered in the test.	☐	☐	☐	☐	☐

SOURCE: From Suinn (1971a). Reprinted with the permission of Richard M. Suinn, Ph.D. All rights reserved.

so on. In addition to the simple sum, the only other scores available are **percentile ranks** (PRs).

The PRs are given in a series of three norms tables; norms are provided separately for total group, for class (i.e., freshman, sophomore, junior, senior), and for sex within each class. Specific instructions on how to use the norms tables to obtain the PRs, along with other information on the psychometric characteristics of the STABS presented later in this section, is found in a manual accompanying the test, *Information for Users* (Suinn, 1971b).

One drawback of the PRs is that they are only given for various score points. Thus, only PRs of 10, 20, 25, 35, 50, 60, 75, 80, and 95 are printed; presumably, other PRs could be calculated through user interpolation. Another limitation of the norms provided for the STABS is that the sample of students the norms are based on was relatively small ($n = 725$). In addition, no description of the characteristics of the norming sample is provided in the technical documentation accompanying the STABS, so potential users cannot ascertain the extent to which the norms would be appropriate for the intended use. Nonetheless, we suspect that the STABS would be helpful and accurate at least for identifying the most and least test-anxious students in a group and for narrowing down those for whom intervention would be most beneficial.

Only a small amount of reliability evidence is provided for the STABS, though the information is helpful. The reliability of scores on the STABS was gauged by giving the test twice to the same groups of students 4 and 6 weeks apart, then calculating a correlation between the two sets of scores. This procedure, known as test-retest reliability or stability, yields a correlation, which, as we learned previously, can be easily interpreted. If the correlation yielded by the test-retest procedure were near its maximum ($r = 1.0$), that would indicate that the scores from the same students obtained weeks apart were perfectly related. That is, the scores would be highly consistent: students who were ranked as having high test anxiety were the same ones identified as having high test anxiety weeks later; conversely, students identified as having the lowest test anxiety would again be identified as having the lowest levels of test anxiety when retested. However, a test-retest reliability correlation of closer to the minimum value ($r = 0.0$) would indicate that students' scores from the first time they were administered the test-anxiety instrument were completely unrelated to the scores they received the second time. Obviously, if a test were truly a good measure of a stable characteristic like test anxiety, one would expect the test-retest reliability to be closer to 1.0 than to 0.0.

Test-retest reliability was calculated for the STABS in groups of undergraduate students and in a group of graduate students. In one group of undergraduates, the test was administered twice, 4 weeks apart. The test-retest reliability for this group was .78. In a second group tested 6 weeks apart, the reliability was .74. In a group of graduate students tested 6 weeks apart, the reliability was .73. Overall, these reliability estimates indicate that the STABS yields fairly consistent scores over time.

Concerning the validity of the STABS, a similarly sparse amount of information is provided in the technical documentation. Validity evidence was gathered based on the theoretical premise that test-anxiety level should be negatively related to course grades (i.e., lower course grades should be obtained for students with higher levels of test anxiety, compared to students with lower levels of test anxiety). In this case, a correlation—the statistical jack-of-all-trades—could be calculated between the two variables such as test-anxiety level and grades. When used this way, correlation would provide what is called a validity coefficient, which would be interpreted in much the same way as any correlation we have already seen. The one critical distinction, however, would be that whether a positive or negative validity coefficient were "good" or "bad" would depend on what relationship between the two variables was expected. For example, as noted previously in this paragraph, we would consider the correlation to be validity evidence supporting the use of the STABS if the correlation were negative (i.e., if lower course grades were associated with higher levels of test anxiety).

No details of the group of students participating in the validity study is provided, beyond that they were enrolled in an introductory psychology course. A correlation was calculated between final grades in the course and STABS scores. As expected, the correlation—that is, the validity coefficient—was negative ($r = -0.26$). A correlation was also calculated between number of errors students made in course examinations and their STABS scores. As would be predicted, this correlation was positive ($r = .24$); that is, students with higher levels of test anxiety made more errors.

A final piece of validity evidence was gathered by correlating scores on the STABS with scores on another test-anxiety instrument, the *Test Anxiety Scale* (Sarason, 1958). In a sample of students, the moderately strong, positive, correlation between the two sets of scores ($r = 0.60$) suggests that the two instruments are, to a fair degree, measuring the same characteristic. Unfortunately, the size and characteristics of the sample on which this validity evidence was gathered are not given.

In addition to the validity information appearing in the STABS technical manual, validity data have also been presented in a separate journal article written by the author of the STABS (Suinn, 1969). In that article, Suinn provides two norms tables, one for a sample of students attending a Hawaiian university and another for a sample attending a Colorado university. In both tables, two sets of PRs are given for both samples; one set of PRs refers to the first time the STABS was administered to the groups, the second refers to the second administration.

The norms data presented in the article suggest some weakness in the validity evidence. Of some concern is the fact that scores on the STABS are uniformly (and fairly substantially) lower when students take the STABS the second time. No intervention for test anxiety was provided to the participants in the study. Thus, if the STABS were truly measuring a stable characteristic such as test anxiety, one would have predicted scores to remain fairly similar. Of greater concern, however, is the fact that the two norms tables give such widely different PRs for the two groups. For example, norms from the second administration indicate that a Hawaiian student would be classified as in the 50th percentile (i.e., "average") with a raw score on the

STABS of 135, whereas the 50th percentile would be assigned to a student from Colorado whose raw score was only 114. Clearly, the norms for the STABS are dependent upon the particular sample and must be used with great caution.

A single independent review of the STABS was published in the eighth edition of the *Mental Measurements Yearbook* (Endler, 1978). Primarily due to the extent to which relevant information is not provided in the technical documentation for the STABS, and because of concerns about the validity of the scores on the instrument, the reviewer was justifiably reluctant to endorse use of the STABS.

The *Test Anxiety Profile* (TAP)

The TAP is another instrument intended to measure test anxiety aligned with current theoretical notions; that is, it is designed to provide separate measures of the worry and emotionality components of test anxiety. A unique feature of the TAP is that it provides further differentiation of test anxiety according to specific types of testing.

The instrument was developed and normed primarily using samples of college students. However, separate norms are provided for high school students, and the wording of items, directions, and so forth suggests that it should easily be used to assess test anxiety in adolescents. It is likely that any high school- or college-aged student could complete the TAP in less than 30 minutes.

The instrument consists of 66 descriptions of various test situations. Each description is accompanied by two bipolar adjectives anchoring two ends of a continuum. Respondents are instructed to check one of seven points along the continuum that best describes them. The 66 statements are arranged into six sets of 11 items that relate to different kinds of test situations. The six test situations (called test types in the TAP manual) covered are multiple-choice exams, essay exams, pop quizzes, tests with math problems, giving a talk in front of the class, and tests with time limits. An optional seventh set of 11 items is included at the end of the TAP for customized use to assess a different test situation.

Each set of 11 items is further broken down into one 5-item set dealing with feelings of anxiety and a 6-item set that addresses anxiety-related thoughts. The TAP is suitable for individual or group administration and should take less than 30 minutes for nearly all students to complete. Directions for administering the instrument and sample statements are reproduced in Figure C–2.

Figure C–2   Sample Items from the *Test Anxiety Profile*

Directions: Sometimes, because of your experiences, a situation will cause negative or positive feelings. On the following pages, you are asked how a particular type of test makes you feel. For example, if the question is about how you feel when taking a test where there is a lot of noise it would be asked in the following way:

[Practice Items]

How I Feel While Trying to Take a Test in Noisy Conditions

(ME)

TENSE_____ :_____ : _____ :_____ : _____ :_____ : _____RELAXED

(BREATHING)

SHALLOW_____ :_____ : _____ :_____ : _____ :_____ : _____DEEP

Imagine that you are taking a test with a lot of noise going on. How would you check the above scales? When taking a test under noisy conditions, how would you use the first pair of adjectives to describe yourself (ME)? Are you TENSE or RELAXED? Are you just a little one way or the other—a lot—or are you neither? (You would check the middle position if you are neither.) Next, how about your breathing? Does it seem to be SHALLOW or DEEP? You have to use your imagination to put yourself in the situation, then look at each word and check the space between the adjectives that best indicates your own response.

[Actual Items]

How I Feel While Taking a Multiple-Choice Exam

(ME)

CALM_____ : _____ : _____ : _____ : _____ : _____ : _____JITTERY

(FINGERS)

STIFF_____ : _____ : _____ : _____ : _____ : _____ : _____RELAXED

(ME)

HELPLESS_____ : _____ : _____ : _____ : _____ : _____ : _____SECURE

(BREATHING)

LOOSE_____ : _____ : _____ : _____ : _____ : _____ : _____TIGHT

(ME)

WORRIED_____ : _____ : _____ : _____ : _____ : _____ : _____CAREFREE

What My Thoughts Are Like While Taking a Multiple-Choice Exam

(IDEAS)

CLEAR_____ :_____ : _____ :_____ : _____ : _____ : _____CONFUSED

(ME)

UNSURE_____ : _____ : _____ : _____ : _____ : _____ : _____SURE

(NOW)

SAFE_____ : _____ : _____ : _____ : _____ : _____ : _____DANGEROUS

(PREPARED)

UNREADY_____ : _____ : _____ : _____ : _____ : _____ : _____READY

(THOUGHTS)

JUMBLED_____ : _____ : _____ : _____ : _____ : _____ : _____EASY

(MIND)

WORKING_____ : _____ : _____ : _____ : _____ : _____ : _____BLANK

SOURCE: From Oetting and Cole (1980). Used by permission.

Administration of the TAP yields scores on two subscales related to the major hypothesized components of test anxiety: feelings of anxiety (FA), related to the emotionality component and designed to assess perceived levels of stress experienced during testing; and thought interference (TI), related to the worry component and designed to assess the thoughts and ideas test takers have during a test.

Scoring the TAP is easily accomplished using a transparent overlay with the weights for each statement (ranging from 1 to 7) printed on the transparency. To obtain raw scores associated with each of the six types of testing, the transparent overlay is placed directly on the student's answer sheet and the weights corresponding to the responses to each item are summed. The sum of the item scores in each 5-item set related to feelings yields an FA subscore for each of the six kinds of testing; raw scores for FA for each testing situation can range from 6 to 35. The sum of the item scores in the 6-item sets measuring cognition yields a TI subscore for type of testing; raw scores for TI for each group of items describing a test situation can range from 7 to 42.

The raw FA and TI subscores are then transferred to a profile sheet that, when the raw scores are plotted, reveals whether the score represents a "high" or "average" level of FA or TI test anxiety for each test situation. The raw scores for a particular testing situation can also be interpreted via narrative descriptions for various raw score ranges, provided in the manual for the TAP. Table C–1 illustrates examples of the score interpretation narratives.

The manual for the TAP emphasizes that raw scores and corresponding narrative interpretations or FA and TI levels for each testing situation are the most valuable data yielded by the TAP. However, norms tables are also provided so that raw scores can be translated into norm-referenced scores (PRs). Separate norms tables are provided

Table C–1   Sample Raw Score Interpretation Narratives for the TAP

FA Scale *Raw Score Intervals*	*Interpretation*
5–9	The testing situation is highly reinforcing and pleasant.
10–14	The student is comfortable in the situation; generally pleasant.
. . .	
26–30	High feelings of anxiety.
31–35	Very high feelings of anxiety, severe problems, approaching phobia.

TI Scale *Raw Score Intervals*	*Interpretation*
6–11	Very great confidence in ability to take test.
12–17	Generally secure and confident.
. . .	
31–36	High thought interference.
37–42	Very high thought interference, severe problems. Person may experience confusion and disorientation in this situation.

SOURCE: Adapted from Oetting and Deffenbacher (1980).

for each of the six testing situations, and norms are given separately for high school and college levels, for each sex, and for total group. Additional information on how to use the norms tables to obtain the PRs, along with other information on the psychometric characteristics of the TAP (presented later in this section), is found in a manual accompanying the test, *Manual: Test Anxiety Profile* (Oetting & Deffenbacher, 1980).

According to the technical manual, college-student norms were based on 628 students ($n = 283$ male, $n = 345$ female) enrolled in introductory psychology classes at Colorado State University. High school norms were derived based on the responses of 61 ninth- through twelfth-grade students enrolled in a single high school serving a small town (population 5,000) and the surrounding agricultural community. No additional information regarding the demographic characteristics of the samples or how they were selected is provided. Although the number of students in the college sample may be large enough, the small sample of high school students results in gaps in the norms tables for that group. For example, on the TI subscale for multiple choice exams, 22 of the 42 possible raw scores had no students in the norm group obtaining that score.

Reliability information is provided for each of the types of testing situation, broken down by the FA and TI subscales. The reliability information must be interpreted with extreme caution, however, as the manual indicates that it was collected on a previous version of the TAP and does not necessarily represent the reliability that would be expected on the current form. Apparently, two portions of a previous form were deleted from the test (those portions dealt with two different testing situations: studying for a test, and taking an oral exam). The first of the two portions was dropped entirely; the second was replaced with the current portions dealing with giving a talk in front of class. Clearly it would be desirable to have reliability information based on the test as currently configured.

Nonetheless, the reliability coefficients for FA and TI are uniformly high. The particular reliability coefficients reported for the TAP are called internal consistency reliability estimates. These are not the same as the test-retest reliability estimates described previously; they are not calculated in the same way (i.e., using correlation), and they are interpreted differently.

The coefficients reported for the TAP are calculated using a method called alpha coefficients. Alpha coefficients (and other similar reliability estimates such as KR-20 and KR-21) are used to express the extent to which the items in an instrument are related to one another; hence, this type of reliability estimate is called internal consistency. The more the items in an instrument are related to each other, the higher the reliability. Theoretically, a test that is highly internally consistent should produce dependable—that is, reliable—results. And happily, alpha reliability estimates are expressed in the same range as other reliability estimates. An alpha coefficient of 1.0 would indicate perfect internal consistency; a coefficient of 0.0 would indicate totally inconsistent results.

Alpha reliability coefficients for the FA subscores on the TAP range from .88 to .96 for each of the six types of testing. The lowest FA reliability is associated with the multiple-choice test situation; the highest is associated with mathematics tests. On the TI subscale, reliabilities ranged from .89 (pop quizzes) to .96 (mathematics).

Test-retest reliability estimates were also calculated for the TAP by administering the instrument to 99 college students at the beginning of a semester, then administering the instrument again to the same students 7 to 10 weeks later. On the FA subscale, test-retest correlations ranged from .66 (essay tests) to .77 (mathematics); on the TI subscale, the correlations ranged from .73 (both essay tests and timed tests) to .81 (oral exams).

Taken together, the fairly high test-retest reliability estimates and the uniformly high internal consistency estimates indicate that scores on the TAP are likely very dependable estimates of a student's level of test anxiety.

Validity evidence for the TAP was gathered in several ways. A primary source of validity evidence is called **construct validity** evidence. The term *construct validity* derives from the notion of a construct, which is simply a generic term for whatever characteristic is measured by a test. Gathering construct validity evidence involves demonstrating that the instrument is well aligned with accepted theories about the characteristic, and demonstrating that scores on the instrument truly reflect varying degrees of the characteristic. Some of the sources of construct validity evidence for the TAP include the design of the instrument according to the two-component theory of test anxiety, development and review of items in the TAP by experts in test anxiety, and results of various research studies. For example, one such study involved administering the TAP to students who came to a college counseling center for test anxiety and received intervention from specialists to help with that problem. The TAP was administered to the students both before and after intervention; as would be expected of a valid instrument, TAP scores were high prior to intervention and lower afterward. In another study, the TAP was administered to students on several consecutive days prior to a test, then once following a test. As would be predicted, test-anxiety scores followed a gradual upward trend, peaking just before the test and dropping immediately afterward.

Recounting in detail all of the construct evidence gathered for the TAP is beyond the scope of this book. However, the manual for the TAP provides ample description of the theoretical basis of test anxiety on which the TAP is based, as well as other evidence that the TAP measures test anxiety and some other, related, constructs. Interested readers may wish to read more about construct validation directly in the TAP manual (Oetting & Deffenbacher, 1980).

A second type of validity evidence gathered for the TAP consists of what is called **convergent validity** evidence. Convergent validity evidence is based on the premise that two tests that truly measure the same characteristic should yield (for the same persons taking both tests) scores that are highly correlated. In the case of a new test such as the TAP, a convergent validity coefficient is calculated (again, correlation is used) to determine the extent to which students' scores on the new test rank them in the same way as their scores on an existing test that is accepted as measuring test anxiety.

To gather convergent validity evidence for the TAP, the correlation was based on scores for a sample of 627 students who took both the TAP and an existing test (in this case, the *Test Anxiety Scale* [TAS]; Sarason, 1972). Scores on each of the 12 separate component-by-type combinations of the TAP were correlated with total scores on the TAS. Examples of component-by-type combinations include the TI score for the pop quiz situation, the FA score for the pop quiz, TI/multiple choice, FA/multiple choice, and so on. These correlations ranged from a low of .27 (TI/oral exam) to .59 (TI/timed test). Because each of these combinations comprises only 5 to 6 items on the TAP, correlations between .30 and .60 actually represent fairly good validity evidence. When all of the component-by-type subscores from the TAP are used in the correlation, multiple correlation with total score on the TAS is .72.

Two independent reviews of the TAP have been published in the *Mental Measurements Yearbook* (see Brown, 1985; Galassi, 1985a). Galassi concluded:

> The TAP represents an intriguing situation-specific approach to test anxiety assessment. Potentially, it is much more versatile than previously devised measures. However, additional data and a much more situationally-specific validation effort is needed before its adequacy can be determined. (1985a, p. 1546)

The *Test Anxiety Inventory* (TAI)

The TAI was developed by one of the leading researchers on test anxiety, Charles Spielberger (1977). The TAI is also sometimes referred to as the *Test Attitude Inventory,* and that is the title actually printed on the instrument given to students. According to the manual accompanying the instrument, it is preferable to refer to the TAI as an attitude instrument and to avoid using the term *anxiety* when administering the TAI to students.

The TAI provides not only a global measure of test anxiety but also a separate measurement of the theoretically relevant worry and emotionality components. The instrument consists of 20 items formatted on a single page, and was developed and normed to be used with high school and college students. According to information provided with the TAI, it has also been used successfully with junior high school students. Translations of the TAI into Dutch, German, and Spanish are available from the publisher, as is a translation into Hebrew from another source (Zeidner, Nevo, & Liefshitz, 1988).

The items on the TAI comprise brief statements of self-descriptions related to testing. Respondents choose one of four options to reflect the extent to which the statement describes them. According to the directions for test, respondents are instructed to darken, for each statement, the bubble next to the choice that describes "how you generally feel" (Spielberger, 1977, p. 1). The four Likert-type choices are *almost never, sometimes, often,* and *almost always.* The complete directions and four sample self-description statements are reproduced in Figure C–3.

The TAI can be administered to students individually via paper and pencil or in groups using machine-scoreable type answer sheets. The manual indicates that high school and college students take approximately 8 to 10 minutes to complete the inventory. A total score on the TAI is obtained by simply summing responses. For items 2 through 20, each of which represents a test-anxious self-description, responses of *almost never* count 1, *sometimes* counts 2, *often* counts 3, and *almost always* counts 4. For Item 1, which describes a confident attitude (i.e., low test anxiety), the scoring is reversed, so that a response of *almost never* counts 4, and so on.

Total scores on the TAI can range from 20 to 80. In addition to a total score, worry and emotionality subscores also can be obtained by summing the respective items in the scale related to those components. Worry and emotionality are each measured by 8 items; thus, scores on each of those subscales range from 8 to 32.

Figure C–3   Sample Items from the *Test Anxiety Inventory*

Directions: A number of statements which people have used to describe themselves are given below. Read each statement and then blacken in the appropriate circle to the right of the statement to indicate how you *generally* feel. There are no right or wrong answers. Do not spend too much time on any one statement, but give the answer which seems to describe how you generally feel.

	Almost Never	Sometimes	Often	Almost Always
1. I feel confident and relaxed while taking tests.	O	O	O	O
2. While taking examinations, I have an uneasy, upset feeling.	O	O	O	O
4. I freeze up on important exams.	O	O	O	O
24. During tests I find myself thinking about the consequences of failing.	O	O	O	O

SOURCE: From Spielberger (1977). Reproduced by special permission of the Publisher, Mind Garden, Inc., 1690 Woodside Road #202, Redwood City, CA 94061 USA www.mindgarden.com. Copyright © 1980 by Charles D. Spielberger. All rights reserved. Further reproduction is prohibited without the Publisher's written consent.

The primary scores of interest from the TAI are the percentile ranks, which allow interpretations of whether a student's test-anxiety level is greater than, less than, or approximately average compared to the student's norm group. PRs are easily obtained directly from the summed raw scores using norms tables provided in the TAI manual. Separate PR norms tables are provided for each of the groups on which the TAI was normed (i.e., high school students, college freshman, community college students, college undergraduates, and naval personnel). PRs are listed for each possible total raw score; separate PR tables are provided for obtaining PRs for the worry and the emotionality subscales. Each of the norms table provides PRs for males and females. The TAI manual provides some additional information on the samples on which the TAI was normed, including sample sizes, sample composition by gender, and time periods and locations of data collection.

Reliability evidence for the TAI consists of both internal consistency coefficients and test-retest reliability estimates. In each of the five norming samples (identified previously), internal consistency estimates (i.e., alpha coefficients) were calculated separately for males and females and are presented in Table C–2. For all groups, the TAI total scores, as well as subscores for worry and emotionality appear to be highly reliable. TAI scores are also very dependable over time, as evidenced by the test-retest correlations reported in the manual. Four test-retest procedures were conducted, with two groups of high-school students and one group each of undergraduate and graduate students taking the TAI at intervals of 2 weeks, 3 weeks, 4 weeks, and 6 months apart. The test-retest correlations for these intervals were .80, .80, .81, and .62, respectively.

Validity evidence supporting interpretations of TAI scores begins with attention to the theory and construct of test anxiety that guided the development of the instrument. According to the manual, "Worry and emotionality may also be thought of as major components of the state-anxiety reactions experienced in test situations. . . . The construction and development of the TAI was [sic] guided by these concepts of worry and emotionality" (Spielberger, 1980, p. 5).

Validity evidence was accrued using a statistical procedure called factor analysis during the development of the TAI. Factor analysis is a procedure that describes the relationship between a total group of items on an instrument and the extent to which the items clump together into what are called factors.[1] Ideally, for a test such as the TAI, it would be desirable not only for factor analysis of all items in the instrument to measure a single construct (i.e., test anxiety) but also for the items to differentiate into two clumps or factors based on the way the TAI had been developed. In this case, the developers intended that the TAI measure the separate factors of worry and emotionality. Thus, validity evidence resulting from factor analysis should show all items measuring a single construct, and those items clumping into two distinct sets.

Initially, a set of 22 items was included in a preliminary factor analysis that was conducted during instrument development. Based on that analysis, two items were deleted which did not clump with other items as intended, resulting in a final set of 20 items that forms the TAI. A separate study using factor analysis and a large sample of college students ($n = 752$) found that the items on the TAI clustered into the two hypothesized factors of worry and emotionality and that those clusterings did not vary across males and females (Ware, Galassi, & Dew, 1990).

Additional validity evidence consists of what are termed item-total correlations, provided in the TAI manual (Spielberger, 1980). These correlations, one for each of the 20 items, indicate the extent of the relationship between scores on each item and total scores on the TAI. Ideally, scores on each item on the TAI should be strongly related to the overall score, if the total score is to be taken as a measure of the characteristic it intends to capture. The TAI manual reports these

Table C–2   Internal Consistency Reliability Estimates for the TAI

	Norm Groups									
	High School		College Freshmen		Community College		College Undergraduate		Naval Recruits	
	Males	Females	Males	Females	Males	Females	Males	Females	Males	Females
TAI Total Score	.92	.93	.92	.93	.93	.96	.94	.95	.94	NA
Worry Subscore	.86	.89	.83	.83	.87	.91	.88	.90	.88	NA
Emotionality Subscore	.90	.91	.85	.87	.89	.91	.90	.91	.85	NA

SOURCE: Adapted from Spielberger (1980)

correlations as observed in groups of high school students ($n = 416$), college freshman ($n = 1,129$), community college students ($n = 246$), college undergraduates ($n = 1449$), and naval personnel ($n = 190$). For all of these samples (except the naval personnel, who were exclusively male), the groups were approximately evenly represented by males and females. The item-total correlations for all 20 items are uniformly high and positive, with median correlations for all groups ranging from .61 to .69.

Convergent validity evidence for the TAI was gathered by administering that instrument to 300 college undergraduates (115 males, 185 females) and also administering other test-anxiety instruments to them concurrently. The other instruments included the *Test Anxiety Scale* (Sarason, 1978), the *State-Trait Anxiety Inventory* (Spielberger, Gorsuch, & Luschene, 1970)—a measure of general anxiety—and the *Worry and Emotionality Questionnaire* (Liebert & Morris, 1967). As would be predicted if the TAI measured the construct of test anxiety, scores on the TAI correlated strongly and positively with scores on the other test-anxiety instruments, and strongly but less positively with scores on the general anxiety measures.

Finally, validity of TAI scores can be evaluated in light of what current theory about test anxiety would predict. As has been found repeatedly in studies of test anxiety, females tend to exhibit higher levels of the characteristic, on average, than do males (see Chapter 4). Data collected during norming of the TAI revealed that total scores on the TAI for females were consistently higher than those of males by approximately 3 to 5 raw score points. These findings also support the validity of the TAI.

A single independent review of the TAI has been published in the *Mental Measurements Yearbook*. Interested readers are referred to Galassi (1985b) for his analysis and critique of the instrument.

The *Children's Test Anxiety Scale* (CTAS)

The most recently developed instrument for measuring test anxiety is the CTAS (Wren & Benson, 2001). After a lull in the development of new test-anxiety instruments in the 1980s and 1990s, Wren and Benson embarked on a test-development project in response to the "increased testing in the elementary schools for children aged 6–12" (p. 1). And because most other existing test-anxiety instruments are intended for use with older students, the CTAS fills a need for a psychometrically sound instrument for measuring test anxiety in a very young population. According to the authors of the CTAS, the other major instrument designed for elementary school–aged children, the *Test Anxiety Scale for Children* (TASC) (Sarason, Davidson, Lighthall, Waite, & Ruebush, 1960), is not appropriate for current use because of its "questionable validity and dated language" (p. 1). Other authors also have observed that the TASC contains wording that may be too complex for young children (Wigfield & Eccles, 1989). For example, one item on the TASC asks, "If you are absent from school and miss an assignment, how much do you worry that you will be behind the other students when you come back to school?" Finally, the authors of the CTAS wanted to produce an instrument that could be used with the increasingly diverse population of students found in U.S. elementary schools—a goal not necessarily pursued by developers of previous instruments.

The CTAS consists of 30 short, linguistically simple statements about a student's thoughts, feelings, and actions in testing situations. The developers of the CTAS report that it is written at the third-grade level. Indeed, the items on the CTAS have their origin in a survey of third-, fourth-, fifth-, and sixth-grade students who were asked open-ended questions regarding their ideas and observations about the characteristics of students who get nervous about testing. The group of students surveyed was diverse, consisting of approximately 50% White students, 30% African American students, and 20% Asian students. All items were reviewed for relevance to measuring test anxiety and age-appropriateness by teachers with at least 5 years of experience with students at the third- to sixth-grade levels.

The CTAS can be administered individually or in a group setting (e.g., the classroom). Regardless of the type of administration, directions for the CTAS should probably be read by a teacher or appropriately qualified adult. Once assured that the respondents understand the directions, students as young as second-grade level should easily be able to read the items in the CTAS and to complete the instrument independently within 5 to 12 minutes.

For each of the statements on the CTAS, respondents choose one of four options. According to the test directions, respondents are instructed to circle one of the four options depending on whether they believe they exhibit the particular thought, feeling, or action *almost never, some of the time, most of the time,* or *almost always* during a test. Figure C–4 provides the complete directions and five sample thought/feeling/action statements from the CTAS.

The reliability of the CTAS was estimated using data collected on 261 elementary school students (46 third-graders, 55 fourth-graders,

Figure C–4   Sample Items from the *Children's Test Anxiety Scale*

Directions: The items describe how some students may think, feel, or act while they are taking tests. Please read each statement carefully and decide if the statement describes how you think, feel, or act **during a test**. Then circle the answer that best describes the way you are while taking a test. If you are not sure which answer to circle, read the statement again before circling your answer.

	Almost never	Some of the time	Most of the time	Almost always
While I am taking tests . . .				
1. I wonder if I will pass.	1	2	3	4
2. My heart beats fast.	1	2	3	4
3. I look around the room.	1	2	3	4
4. I feel nervous.	1	2	3	4
5. I think I am going to get a bad grade.	1	2	3	4

SOURCE: Adapted from Wren and Benson (2001).

94 fifth-graders, and 66 sixth-graders) from four different schools. Although the characteristics of the schools and the demographic characteristics of the students are not well described, the authors indicate that the sample was 47% males and 53% females, and that the ethnic composition of the sample was approximately 51% White, 44% African American, and 5% Asian.

The internal consistency reliability estimate (i.e., alpha coefficients) for the total sample using total scores on the CTAS was very high ($r = .92$). As would be predicted, reliability generally increased when examined separately across Grades 3 through 6, with alpha coefficients of .88, .92, .93, and .91, respectively. The CTAS yields scores that are virtually as reliable for boys as for girls ($r = .90$ and .92, respectively), and the reliability estimates for ethnic groups were also high and homogenous ($r = .89, .90$, and .92 for Asian, African American, and White groups, respectively). No other reliability information (such as test-retest reliability) is available for the CTAS.

Validity evidence for the CTAS necessarily begins with construct validity. As with other measures based on current theories of test anxiety, the CTAS reflects the two-component (emotionality and worry) conceptualization of test anxiety. The authors indicate that the CTAS reflects a view of test anxiety as "a situation-specific trait which occurs during formal evaluative situations and is experienced as an unpleasant emotional state, with accompanying cognitions, somatic symptoms, and behaviors" (Wren & Benson, 2001, p. 5). For their purposes, the authors of the CTAS re-labeled the emotionality component as *autonomic reactions.* The authors also expanded the worry component and re-labeled it *thoughts.* According to the authors, "the *thoughts* component we are proposing as a part of children's test anxiety includes not only the various worry cognitions that occur during testing, but also self-critical thoughts, test-related concerns, and test-irrelevant thoughts" (p. 6). Finally the authors include a third component, which they call test-irrelevant behaviors. This expanded conceptualization is better aligned to the transactional model of test anxiety described in Chapter 2 of this book.

Though beyond the scope of this book, validity evidence for the CTAS was also gathered using factor-analytic and cross-validation procedures. Interested readers are referred to the source (Wren & Benson, 2001) for detailed description of these procedures and results. Finally, because the CTAS is still relatively new and is undergoing additional revision and development, independent reviews of the CTAS are not available in *MMY.*

The *FRIEDBEN Test Anxiety Scale* (FTAS)

Among the newest instruments for measuring test anxiety is the FTAS. The name of the instrument (FRIEDBEN) is derived from a combination of the last names of the instrument's authors (Friedman & Bendas-Jacob, 1997). Although the FTAS is not commercially available or yet reviewed in *MMY,* the instrument itself and relevant technical information about the instrument's development and validation are found in the research article that originally introduced it. It is notable that the FTAS attempts to advance both the measurement and theory of test anxiety.

The FTAS consists of 23 items designed to measure test anxiety in adolescents (i.e., middle school– or junior high school–aged students). Each item is a statement related to testing. Students respond to the statements by indicating the degree to which the statement describes them, using a scale that ranges from 1 (the statement does not characterize the student at all) to 6 (the statement characterizes the student perfectly). Directions for administering and scoring the FTAS are not available; however, all items for the instrument are provided in Figure C–5.

Figure C–5   The *FRIEDBEN Test Anxiety Scale*

	Does Not Characterize Me at All			Characterizes Me Perfectly		
	1	2	3	4	5	6
1. If I fail a test I am afraid I shall be rated as stupid by my friends.	1	2	3	4	5	6
2. If I fail a test I am afraid people will consider me worthless.	1	2	3	4	5	6
3. If I fail a test I am afraid my teachers will derogate me.	1	2	3	4	5	6
4. If I fail a test I am afraid my teachers will believe I am hopelessly dumb.	1	2	3	4	5	6
5. I am very worried about what my teacher will think or do if I fail his or her test.	1	2	3	4	5	6
6. I am worried that all my friends will get high scores on the test and only I will get low ones.	1	2	3	4	5	6
7. I am worried that failure in tests will embarrass me socially.	1	2	3	4	5	6
8. I am worried that if I fail a test my parents will not like it.	1	2	3	4	5	6
9. During a test my thoughts are clear and I neatly answer all questions.	1	2	3	4	5	6
10. During a test I feel I'm in good shape and that I'm organized.	1	2	3	4	5	6
11. I feel my chances are good to think and perform well on tests.	1	2	3	4	5	6
12. I usually function well on tests.	1	2	3	4	5	6
13. I feel I just can't make it on tests.	1	2	3	4	5	6
14. In a test I feel like my head is empty, as if I have forgotten all I have learned.	1	2	3	4	5	6
15. During a test it's hard for me to organize what's in my head in an orderly fashion.	1	2	3	4	5	6

	Does Not Characterize Me at All			Characterizes Me Perfectly		
	1	2	3	4	5	6
16. I feel it is useless for me to sit for an examination, I shall fail no matter what.	1	2	3	4	5	6
17. Before a test it is clear to me that I'll fail no matter how well prepared I am.	1	2	3	4	5	6
18. I am very tense before a test, even if I am well prepared.	1	2	3	4	5	6
19. While I am sitting in an important test, I feel that my heart pounds strongly.	1	2	3	4	5	6
20. During a test my whole body is very tense.	1	2	3	4	5	6
21. I am terribly scared of tests.	1	2	3	4	5	6
22. During a test I keep moving uneasily in my chair.	1	2	3	4	5	6
23. I arrive at a test with no serious tension or nervousness.	1	2	3	4	5	6

SOURCE: From Friedman and Benadas-Jacob (1997). Used with permission.

Development of the FTAS began by surveying 80 high school students who were asked open-ended questions such as "What does a student whom you would define as suffering from test anxiety think and feel?" and "How would a student suffering from test anxiety behave before, during, and after a test?" (Friedman & Bendas-Jacob, 1997, p. 1038). The students' responses were analyzed for commonalities, and a final set of 23 items in three categories was developed. The three categories, which also name the three subscales of the FTAS are (a) social derogation, defined by the authors as describing "the student's apprehension of what people will say if people learn that the student has failed" (p. 1041) and represented by items 1 through 8 in Figure C–5; (b) cognitive obstruction, which refers to the student "not being able to perform adequately during a test, being unable to organize thoughts in an orderly fashion, or being unable to operate intelligently in a test situation" (p. 1041), represented by items 9 through 17 in Figure C–5; and (c) tenseness, which is defined as "the student's sense of nervousness before or during a test" (p. 1041) and is represented by items 18 to 23 in the figure.

Reliability and validity evidence for the FTAS were obtained using a sample of 1,925 students from 23 junior high and high schools. Internal consistency estimates of reliability (alpha coefficients) were .91 for total scores on the FTAS, and .86, .85, and .81, respectively, for the three subscales described previously. For an instrument of this length, the internal consistency is quite high; additional reliability evidence, such as test-retest information would be desirable.

Convergent validity evidence for the FTAS was obtained by correlating scores on the FTAS instrument with scores on the TAI, which was also administered to a sample of 369 high school students. For both boys and girls, the relationship between the two instruments was strong (.84 and .82, respectively). An interesting second source of convergent validity evidence was obtained by asking 39 students who took the FTAS to also rate the level of stress they believed was experienced by each of their peers in their classrooms. Correlations for these data showed that students whom peers perceived to be highly stressed obtained higher scores on the FTAS ($r = .75$). Finally, in addition to the construct validity evidence obtained during the development of the instrument, statistical evidence from factor analysis (described previously in this appendix) was obtained. Again, while it is beyond the scope of this book, the factor analysis results support the desired interpretation of FTAS scores as indicators of degree of test anxiety.

Overall, the FTAS may portend what test-anxiety instruments of the future will look like. In particular, the three components of test anxiety it measures go beyond the two factors traditionally measured (i.e., worry and emotionality) and suggest that refinement of current theories of test anxiety may be in order. Much additional work and evidence is required for the FTAS, however, before it can be confidently recommended for wider use. For one thing, the instrument may need to be reevaluated for its readability by the intended adolescent audience. It is likely that words used in some of the items (e.g., "derogates" in Item 3) may not be comprehended by middle schoolers.

Other Test Anxiety Instruments

Several other instruments are available for measuring test anxiety, though for various reasons, we will not dwell on them at length here and do not recommend them for current use. Brief descriptions of and comments on these instruments are provided below for the benefit of readers who may encounter references to them in the literature, or actual copies of the instruments in schools, counseling departments, and so on.

An instrument frequently encountered in the professional literature on test anxiety is the previously mentioned *Test Anxiety Scale for Children* (Sarason, Davidson, Lighthall, & Waite, 1958; Sarason, Davidson, Lighthall, Waite, & Ruebush, 1960). The TASC is intended for use with elementary school–aged children in Grades 1 though 9. The TASC is brief, thoroughly researched, and has been modified often since its introduction in 1958. The original version of the TASC began as an instrument comprising 43 questions to which students respond yes or no. The most commonly used version comprises 30 items. Feld and Lewis (1969) have produced a version of the TASC in which the wordings of the items are reversed (i.e., they ask about students' level of comfort instead of their level of anxiety in certain situations). Additionally, they report on the *Expanded Test Anxiety Scale for Children*, which adds two additional items to the original TASC. The two additional items ask if the student thinks about schoolwork at home or dreams about schoolwork at night. Sample items and directions for administering the TASC are shown in Figure C–6.

Figure C–6 Sample Items from the *Test Anxiety Scale for Children*

Directions [read to young students]: "My name is _____. I'm going to be asking you some questions. These are different from the usual school questions for these are about how you feel and so have no right or wrong answers. . . . You are to listen to each question and then put a circle around either 'Yes' or 'No'. . . . "

Yes   No   1. Do you worry when the teacher says that she is going to ask you questions to find out how much you know?

Yes   No   5. Do you sometimes dream at night that you are in school and cannot answer the teacher's questions?

Yes   No   16. When the teacher says that she is going to find out how much you have learned, do you get a funny feeling in your stomach?

Yes   No   19. Are you afraid of tests in school?

Yes   No   26. When you are taking a hard test, do you forget some things that you knew very well before you started taking the test?

NOTES:

1. From Sarason, Davidson, Lighthall, Waite, and Ruebush (1960). Used by permission of Sey mour B. Sarason.

Harnisch, Hill, and Fyans (1980) have produced from the original TASC short, shorter, and shortest forms of the TASC, consisting of subsets of 14, 12, and 7 items, respectively. The versions were field tested on large samples of students in Grades 4, 8, and 11 in Illinois. The authors assert that these versions represent "shorter, more reliable, and more valid measures of test motivation" (p. 1).

Unfortunately, virtually no documentation is available for any versions of the TASC described here. We cannot recommend administration of unproved, undocumented instruments.

Note

1. The following description of factor analysis takes some liberties with the terminology and technical machinations of that procedure. We suspect that few readers would be interested in the details of factor analysis or how it was implemented for gathering validity evidence for the TAI. Readers who are interested in more information on factor analysis in general are referred to short but clear books on the procedure by Kim and Mueller (1978a, 1978b). Additional information on how factor analysis was applied in this case is available in Spielberger (1980).

References

American Educational Research Association [AERA], American Psychological Association [APA], National Council on Measurement in Education [NCME]. (1999). *Standards for educational and psychological testing.* Washington, DC: American Educational Research Association.

Anderson, S. B., & Sauser, Jr., W. I. (1995). Measurement of test anxiety: An overview. In C. D. Spielberger & P. R. Vagg (Eds.), *Test anxiety: Theory, assessment, and treatment* (pp. 15–34). Washington, DC: Taylor & Francis.

Ball, S. (1995). Anxiety and test performance. In C. D. Spielberger & P. Vagg (Eds.), *Test anxiety: Theory, assessment, and treatment* (pp. 107–113). Washington, DC: Taylor & Francis.

Becker, P. (1982). Fear reactions and achievement behavior of students approaching an examination. In H. W. Krohne & L. Laux (Eds.), *Achievement, stress, and anxiety* (pp. 275–290). Washington, DC: Hemisphere.

Beidel, D. C. (1991). Social phobia and overanxious disorder in school-age children. *Journal of the American Academy of Child and Adolescent Psychiatry, 30,* 545–552.

Berliner, D., & Casanova, U. (1988). How do we balance test anxiety and achievement? *Instructor, 97*(8), 14–15.

Brown, S. D. (1985). Review of *Test Anxiety Profile.* In J. V. Mitchell (Ed.), *The ninth mental measurements yearbook* (pp. 1543–1545). Lincoln, NE: University of Nebraska Press.

Carpenter, T. P., & Lehrer, R. (1999). Teaching and learning mathematics with understanding. In E. Fennema & T. A. Romberg (Eds.), *Mathematics classrooms that promote understanding* (pp. 19–32). Mahwah, NJ: Lawrence Erlbaum.

Center for Education Policy (2004, August). *State high school exit exams.* Washington, DC: Author.

Chapell, M. S., & Overton, W. F. (1998). Development of logical reasoning in the context of parenting style and test anxiety. *Merrill-Palmer Quarterly, 44,* 141–152.

Chappuis, S., & Stiggins, R. J. (2002). Classroom assessment for learning. *Educational Leadership, 60*(1), 40–43.

Cizek, G. J. (1995). The big picture in assessment and who ought to have it. *Phi Delta Kappan, 77*(3), 246–249.

Cizek, G. J. (1999). *Cheating on tests: How to do it, detect it, and prevent it.* Mahwah, NJ: Lawrence Erlbaum.

Cizek, G. J. (2001a). Cheating to the test. *Education Matters, 1*(1), 40–47.

Cizek, G. J. (2001b). More unintended consequences of high-stakes testing. *Educational Measurement: Issues and Practice, 20*(4), 19–27.

Cizek, G. J. (2003a). *Detecting and preventing classroom cheating: Promoting integrity in schools.* Thousand Oaks, CA: Corwin.

Cizek, G. J. (2003b). Educational testing integrity: Why educators and students cheat and how to prevent it. In G. R. Walz & J. E. Wall (Eds.), *Measuring up: Assessment issues for teachers, counselors, and administrators* (pp. 363–386). Greensboro, NC: ERIC Counseling and Student Services Clearinghouse.

Cizek, G. J. (2003c). When teachers cheat. *Education Digest, 68*(6), 28–31.

Collins, R. (1979). *The credential society: A historical sociology of education and stratification.* New York: Academic.

Crocker, L., & Algina, J. (1986). *Introduction to classical and modern test theory.* Fort Worth, TX: Holt, Rinehart and Winston.

Crocker, L., Schmitt, A., & Tang, L. (1988). Test anxiety and standardized achievement test performance in the middle school years. *Measurement and Evaluation in Counseling and Development, 20*(4), 149-157.

Donegan, M. M., & Trepanier-Street, M. (1998). Teacher and parent views on standardized testing: A cross-cultural comparison of the uses and influencing factors. *Journal of Research in Childhood Education, 13*(1), 85–93.

Dweck, C. S. (1986). Motivational processes affecting learning. *American Psychologist, 41*(10), 1040–1046.

Ebel, R. L. (1961). Must all tests be valid? *American Psychologist, 16*, 640–647.

Endler, N. S. (1978). Review of *Suinn Test Anxiety Behavior Scale.* In O. K. Buros (Ed.), *The eighth mental measurements yearbook* (pp. 1104–1106). Lincoln, NE: University of Nebraska Press.

Erford, B. T., & Moore-Thomas, C. (2004). Testing FAQ: How to answer questions parents frequently ask about testing. In J. E. Wall & G. R. Walz (Eds.), *Measuring up: Assessment issues for teachers, counselors, and administrators* (pp. 535–555). Greensboro, NC: ERIC Clearinghouse on Counseling and Student Services.

Ergene, T. (2003). Effective interventions for test anxiety reduction: A meta-analysis. *School Psychology International, 24*(3), 313–328.

Eschemann, K. K. (1992). The impact of testing on student motivation. *Journal of Epsilon Pi Tau, 18*(1), 28–32.

Everson, H. T., Tobias, S., Hartman, H., & Gourgey, A. (1991, April). *Test anxiety in different curricular areas: An exploratory analysis of the role of subject matter.* Paper presented at the annual meeting of the American Educational Research Association, Chicago, IL.

Everson, H. T., Tobias, S., Hartman, H., & Gourgey, A. (1993). *Test anxiety and the curriculum: The subject matters.* New York: The College Board.

Feld, S. C., & Lewis, J. L. (1969). The assessment of achievement anxieties in children. In C. P. Smith (Ed.), *Achievement-related motives in children* (pp. 151–199). New York: Russell Sage.

Fleege, P. O., Charlesworth, R., Burts, D. C., & Hart, C. H. (1992). Stress begins in kindergarten: A look at behavior during standardized testing. *Journal of Research in Childhood Education, 7*(1), 20–26.

Friedman, I. A., & Bendas-Jacob, O. (1997). Measuring perceived test anxiety in adolescents: A self-report scale. *Educational and Psychological Measurement, 57*(6), 1035–1046.

Galassi, J. P. (1985a). Review of *Test Anxiety Profile*. In J. V. Mitchell (Ed.), *The ninth mental measurements yearbook* (pp. 1545–1546). Lincoln, NE: University of Nebraska Press.

Galassi, J. P. (1985b). Review of *Test Attitude Inventory*. In J. V. Mitchell (Ed.), *The ninth mental measurements yearbook* (pp. 1547–1548). Lincoln, NE: University of Nebraska Press.

Gilman, D. A., & Reynolds, L. L. (1991). The side effects of statewide testing. *Contemporary Education, 62*(4), 273–278.

Goonan, B. (2004). Overcoming test anxiety: Giving students the ability to show what they know. In J. E. Wall & G. R. Walz (Eds.), *Measuring up: Assessment issues for teachers, counselors, and administrators* (pp. 257–272). Greensboro, NC: ERIC Clearinghouse on Counseling and Student Services.

Greene, J. P., & Winters, M. A. (2004). *Pushed out or pulled up? Exit exams and dropout rates in public high schools* (Education Working Paper No. 5). New York: Manhattan Institute for Policy Research.

Guida, F. V., & Ludlow, L. H. (1989). A cross-cultural study of test anxiety. *Journal of Cross-Cultural Psychology, 20*(2), 178–190.

Guttman, J. (1987). Test anxiety and performance of adolescent children of divorced parents. *Educational Psychology, 7*(3), 225–229.

Haladyna, T. M., Nolen, S. B., & Haas, N. S. (1991). Raising standardized achievement test scores and the origins of test score pollution. *Educational Researcher, 20*(5), 2–7.

Harnisch, D. L., Hill, K. T., & Fyans, Jr., L. J. (1980, April). *Development of a shorter, more reliable, and more valid measure of test motivation.* Paper presented at the annual meeting of the National Council on Measurement in Education, Boston, MA.

Helmke, A. (1988). The role of classroom context factors for the achievement-impairing effect of test anxiety. *Anxiety Research, 1*(1), 37–52.

Hembree, R. (1988). Correlates, causes, effects, and treatment of test anxiety. *Review of Educational Research, 58,* 47–77.

Hill, K. T. (1984). Debilitating motivation and testing: A major educational problem, possible solutions, and policy applications. In R. Ames & C. Ames (Eds.), *Research on motivation in education: Student motivation* (pp. 245–274). Orlando, FL: Academic.

Hill, K. T., & Wigfield, A. (1984). Test anxiety: A major educational problem and what can be done about it. *Elementary School Journal, 85*(1), 106–126.

Hills, J. R. (1991). Apathy concerning grading and testing. *Phi Delta Kappan, 72,* 540–545.

Holt, J. (1982). *How children fail.* New York: Delta.

Hunsley, J. (1985). Test anxiety, academic performance, and cognitive appraisals. *Journal of Educational Psychology, 77,* 678–682.

Jacob, B. A., & Levitt, S. D. (2003). *Rotten apples: An investigation of the prevalence and predictors of teacher cheating* (NBER Working Paper No. W9413). Cambridge, MA: National Bureau of Economic Research.

Joint Committee on Testing Practices. (2000). *Rights and responsibilities of test takers.* Washington, DC: American Psychological Association.

Joint Committee on Testing Practices. (2004). *Code of fair testing practices in education.* Washington, DC: American Psychological Association.

Kim, J., & Mueller, C. W. (1978a). *Factor analysis: Statistical methods and practical issues.* Thousand Oaks, CA: Sage.

Kim, J., & Mueller, C. W. (1978b). *Factor analysis: What it is and how to do it.* Thousand Oaks, CA: Sage.

Liebert, R. M., & Morris, L. W. (1967). Cognitive and emotional components of test anxiety: A distinction and some initial data. *Psychological Reports, 20,* 975–978.

Mandler, G., & Sarason, S. B. (1952). The effects of prior experience and subjective failure on the evocation of test anxiety. *Journal of Personality, 21,* 338–341.

Mass Insight Education. (2002, March). *Taking charge: Urban high school students speak out about MCAS, academics and extra-help programs.* Boston: Author.

McDonald, A. S. (2001). The prevalence and effects of test anxiety in school children. *Educational Psychology: An International Journal of Experimental Educational Psychology, 21*(1), 89–101.

Mealey, D. L., & Host, T. R. (1992). Coping with test anxiety. *College Teaching, 40*(4) 147–150.

Mehrens, W. A. (1991, April). *Defensible/indefensible instructional preparation for high stakes achievement tests.* Paper presented at the annual meeting of the National Council on Measurement in Education, Chicago, IL.

Mehrens, W. A., & Cizek, G. J. (2001). Standard setting and the public good: Benefits accrued and anticipated. In G. J. Cizek (Ed.), *Setting performance standards: Concepts, methods, and perspectives* (pp. 477–485). Mahwah, NJ: Lawrence Erlbaum.

Mehrens, W. A., & Kaminski, J. (1989). Methods for improving standardized test scores: Fruitful, fruitless, or fraudulent? *Educational Measurement: Issues and Practice, 8*(1), 14–22.

Mehrens, W. A., Popham, W. J., & Ryan, J. M. (1998). How to prepare students for performance assessments. *Educational Measurement: Issues and Practice, 17*(1), 18-22.

Messick, S. (1989). Validity. In R. L. Linn (Ed.), *Educational measurement, third edition* (pp. 13–103). New York: Macmillan.

Moke, S., & Shermis, M. (Eds.). (2001). *Success with test-taking.* Bloomington, IN: Family Learning Association.

Monsaas, J. A., & Engelhard, Jr., G. (1994). Teachers' attitudes toward testing practices. *Journal of Psychology, 128,* 469–477.

Mueller, C. M., & Dweck, C. S. (1998). Praise for intelligence can undermine children's motivation and performance. *Journal of Personality and Social Psychology, 75*(1), 33–52.

Mulvenon, S. W., Stegman, C. E., & Ritter, G. (2003, April). *Test anxiety: A multifaceted study on the perceptions of teachers, principals, counselors, students and parents.* Paper presented at the annual meeting of the American Educational Research Association, Chicago, IL.

National Council on Measurement in Education. (1995). *Code of professional responsibilities in educational measurement.* Washington, DC: Author.

Oetting, E. R., & Cole, C. W. (1980). *Test anxiety profile.* Fort Collins, CO: Tri-Ethnic Center for Prevention Research.

Oetting, E. R., & Deffenbacher, J. L. (1980). *Manual: Test anxiety profile.* Fort Collins, CO: Tri-Ethnic Center for Prevention Research.

O'Sullivan, R. G. (1989, February). *Teacher perceptions of the effects of testing on students*. Paper presented at the Annual Meeting of the National Council on Measurement in Education, San Francisco, CA.

Paris, S. G., Lawton, T. A., Turner, J. C., & Roth, J. L. (1991). A developmental perspective on standardized achievement testing. *Educational Researcher, 20*(5), 12–20.

Pedulla, J. J., Abrams, L. M., Madaus, G. F., Russell, M. K., Ramos, M. A., & Miao, J. (2003). *Perceived effects of state-mandated testing programs on teaching and learning: Findings from a national survey of teachers*. Chestnut Hill, MA: National Board on Educational Testing and Public Policy.

Peleg-Popko, O., & Klingman, A. (2002). Family environment, discrepancies between perceived actual and desirable environment, and children's test and trait anxiety. *British Journal of Guidance & Counseling, 30*(4), 451–466.

Principal Accused of "Weeding Out" Students to Raise Scores. (2003). Retrieved June 6, 2004, from http://www.loca110.com/education/2308606/detail.html

Sapp, M. (1999). *Test anxiety: Applied research, assessment, and treatment interventions* (2nd ed.). Lanham, MD: University Press of America.

Sarason, I. G. (1958). The effects of anxiety, reassurance, and meaningfulness of material to be learned on verbal learning. *Journal of Experimental Psychology, 56*, 472–477.

Sarason, I. G. (1972). Experimental approaches to test anxiety: Attention and the uses of information. In C. D. Spielberger (Ed.), *Anxiety: Current trends in theory and research* (pp. 381–403). New York: Academic.

Sarason, I. G. (1978). The *Test Anxiety Scale:* Concept and research. In C. D. Spielberger & I. G. Sarason (Eds.), *Stress and anxiety* (Vol. 5, pp. 193–216). New York: Wiley.

Sarason, I. G. (1981). Test anxiety, stress, and social support. *Journal of Personality, 41*, 101–114.

Sarason, S. B. (1959). What research says about test anxiety in elementary school children. *NEA Journal, 48*, 26–27.

Sarason, S. B., Davidson, K., Lighthall, F., & Waite, R. (1958). A test anxiety scale for children. *Child Development, 29*, 105–113.

Sarason, S. B., Davidson, K. S., Lighthall, F. F., Waite, R. R., & Ruebush, B. K. (1960). *Anxiety in elementary school children: A report of research*. New York: Wiley.

Shermis, M. D., & Lombard, D. (1998). Effects of computer-based test administration on test anxiety and performance. *Computers in Human Behavior, 14*(1), 111–123.

Schmitt, A. P., & Crocker, L. (1982, March). *Measurement of test anxiety for examinees, grades 6-8*. Paper presented at the annual meeting of the American Educational Research Association, New York, NY.

Smith, M. L. (1991). Put to the test: The effects of external testing on teachers. *Educational Researcher, 20*(5), 8–11.

Spielberger, C. D. (1977). *Test anxiety inventory*. Palo Alto, CA: Consulting Psychologists Press.

Spielberger, C. D. (1980). *Test Anxiety Inventory: Preliminary professional manual*. Redwood City, CA: Mindgarden.

Spielberger, C. D., Gonzalez, H. P., Taylor, C. J., Algaze, B., & Anton, W. D. (1978). Examination stress and anxiety. In C. D. Spielberger & I. G. Sarason (Eds.), *Stress and anxiety* (Vol. 5, pp. 167–191). Washington, DC: Hemisphere.

Spielberger, C. D., Gorsuch, R. L., & Luschene, R. E. (1970). *State-Trait Anxiety Inventory.* Palo Alto, CA: Consulting Psychologists Press.

Spielberger, C. D., & Vagg, P. R. (1995). *Test anxiety: Theory, assessment, and treatment.* Washington, DC: Taylor & Francis.

Stiggins, R. J. (1991). Assessment literacy. *Phi Delta Kappan, 72,* 534–539.

Stiggins, R. J. (1995). Assessment literacy for the 21st century. *Phi Delta Kappan, 77,* 238–245.

Stiggins, R. J. (2005). Student-involved assessment for learning. New York: Prentice Hall.

Suinn, R. (1969). The STABS, a measure of test anxiety for behavior therapy: Normative data. *Behaviour Research and Therapy, 1,* 335-339.

Suinn, R. M. (1971a). *Suinn test anxiety behavior scale.* Fort Collins, CO: Rocky Mountain Behavior Science Institute.

Suinn, R. M. (1971b). *Suinn test anxiety behavior scale: Information for users.* Fort Collins, CO: Rocky Mountain Behavior Science Institute.

Sumprer, G. E., & Hollandsworth, J. G. (1982). Effect of weekly tests versus a single mid-term examination on anxiety, task-irrelevant thinking, and test performance. *Behavioral Counseling Quarterly, 2,* 51–57.

Turner, B. G., Beidel, D. C., Hughes, S., & Turner, M. W. (1993). Test anxiety in African American school children. *School Psychology Quarterly, 8*(2), 140–152.

United States General Accounting Office. (1993, January). *Student testing: Current extent and expenditures with cost estimates for a national examination* (Report No. PEMD-93–8). Washington, DC: Author.

Ware, W. B., Galassi, J. P., & Dew, K. M. H. (1990). The Test Anxiety Inventory: A confirmatory factor analysis. *Anxiety Research, 3,* 205–212.

Wigfield, A., & Eccles, J. S. (1989). Test anxiety in elementary and secondary school students. *Educational Psychologist, 24*(2), 159–183.

Wilkinson, C. M. (1990). Techniques for overcoming test anxiety. *Elementary School Guidance & Counseling, 24*(3), 24–27.

Wolf, L. F., & Smith, J. K. (1993, April). *The effects of motivation and anxiety on test performance.* Paper presented at the annual meeting of the American Educational Research Association, Atlanta, GA.

Wren, D. G., & Benson, J. (2001, July). *Development and validation of a children's test anxiety scale.* Paper presented at the annual meeting of the Stress and Anxiety Research Society, Palma de Mallorca, Spain.

Yerkes, R. M., & Dodson, J. D. (1908). The relation of strength of stimulus to rapidity of habit-formation. *Journal of Comparative Neurology and Psychology, 18,* 459–482.

Zeidner, M. (1998). *Test anxiety: The state of the art.* New York City, NY: Plenum.

Zeidner, M., Nevo, B., & Leifshitz, H. (1988). *Test Anxiety Scale: Operating manual.* Haifa, Israel: Haifa University Press.

Zimbardo, P. G., Butler, L. D., & Wolfe, V. A. (2003). Cooperative college examinations: More gain, less pain when students share information and grades. *Journal of Experimental Education, 71*(2), 101–125.

Index